The Florida
One-Day Trip Book

The Florida One-Day Trip Book

52 Off-Beat Excursions In and Around Orlando

Edward Hayes

EPM Publications, Inc.
McLean, Virginia

Library of Congress Cataloging in Publication Data

Hayes, Edward, 1924—
    The Florida one-day trip book

    Includes index.
        1. Orlando (Fla.)—Description—Guide-books.
    2. Orlando Region (Fla.)—Description and travel—Guide-
    books.   I. Title.
    F319.07H38   1985   917.59'24   85-27599
    ISBN 0-914440-89-6

EPM Publications, Inc.
1003 Turkey Run Road
McLean, Virginia 22101
Printed in the United States of America

Book Design and Cover Illustration
by Tom Huestis

To the memory of everyone who tried to get a book published—all those who really worked at it—and never reached that dream. And to Evelyn Metzger and Betty Ann Weber who made this one possible.

Contents

TO THE EAST:

TO THE WEST:

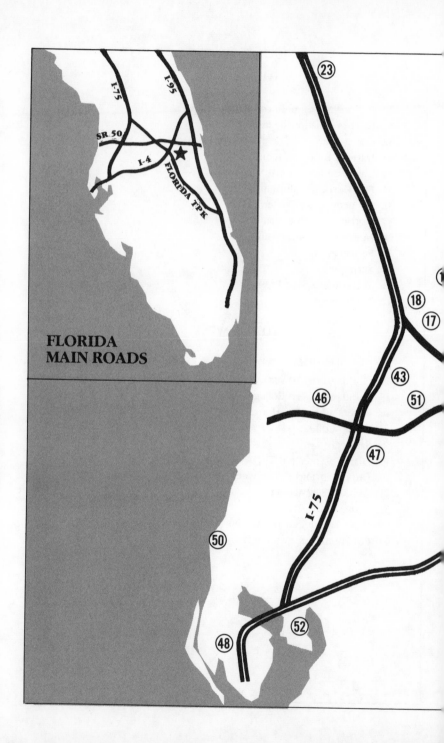

FLORIDA
MAIN ROADS

Lake Eola Fountain at Eola Park, focal point of downtown Orlando. Photo by Bobby Coker.

Once upon a time, long before Walt Disney waved his magic pen and drew a new, permanent face on the map of Florida, Orlando was the hub city of the peninsular state for no reason other than its geographic designation. Once, hugged by citrus groves in all directions, Orlando took justifiable pride in its quiet, boundless treasures of lakes, subtropical climate and unhurried lifestyle; and called itself City Beautiful.

A decade ago, with the birth of Walt Disney World, Central Florida was struck with significant change, both economic and visual. Orlando, situated a few miles up the road from the entrance to Disney's Magic Kingdom, suddenly found itself with a new banner: vacation capital of the world. Not unexpectedly, the fantastic invasion of the Disney fantasies ignited an overnight mushrooming of other multi-million-dollar tourist attractions, hotels and restaurants, drawing domestic and foreign visitors to the area by the million annually.

And now that Disney has opened its colossal Epcot Center, it's like having a world's fair in your town every day of every year.

The motive of this book, however, is not to highlight the headline attractions. Nor, certainly, is it designed to minimize their importance or appeal. After all, what parents, vacationing in Central Florida, would dream of depriving their children of the opportunity to explore the excitement of Disney World; or the chance to be a clown at Circus World; or the unique experience of petting a real live porpoise at Sea World?

These pages, instead, serve reminders that the so-called major attractions represent only a slim fraction of what is to be seen, relished and photographed in the Sunshine State. The simpler, more realistic treasures of nature and history abound. All one needs to know is where, when and why to find them. Adventure: that's the plot of this book. Found in these pages are the off-beat excursions for the enterprising; the mini-vacation for the economy conscious tourist and visitor. These are the fun and frequently educational places and events, some old, some new, mostly unlisted in the official guidebooks—and in many cases overlooked or forgotten by residents themselves.

And they're all reachable in a day's drive from Orlando.

Short on ideas, short on vacation money and time? Jaded by the tinsel, jostled by the crowds? Tired of digging into purse or billfold at every turn? This is your book, a collection of those sightseeing alternatives and retreats for you and your family at half the price. Sometimes there is no charge at all—except for the gasoline you put in your car or camper. On these pages are detailed directions on how to get there, best times to go, and what to expect upon arrival.

This is a book for families, groups, couples and loners.

Weather, naturally, is the state's chief asset, making travel a virtual all-season paradise. But even Florida has its bad days. No problem. A little enterprise goes a long way. Example: The day you promised to drive the family to one of the Atlantic coast beaches turns up chilly or stormy. All this means is that you probably won't want to spend the whole day at the beach; so you check this guide and surprise your family with interesting stopoffs. If Titusville or Cocoa Beach is your destination, for instance, put Christmas in your day also.

Christmas is a small, unincorporated town eighteen miles east of Orlando on State Road 50. Even if you're in a hurry to get to the beach you'll want to pull in at the tiny post office to get the internationally renowned Christmas postmark on your letters and cards. While there, drive a mile north on a well-paved highway to see the replica of Fort Christmas. The original fort, destroyed by fire long ago, was built in 1837, a cooperative effort of the United States Army, pioneers and settlers for protection against the Indians during the Second Seminole War. Inside Fort Christmas (no admission charge) are absorbing examples of weapons, clothing, cooking utensils and the like from that important page of American history. Outside the fort, picnic tables are scattered invitingly beneath the pines.

And so on.

Please bear in mind that times and admission prices herein are subject to change. There might be variance in the mileage listings also because of border expansions and annexations. As you may note later on, the City of Orlando recently extended its official boundary lines to take in Turkey Lake. We expect more of this.

The book begins with thirteen suggested visits in the immediate Orlando area, which includes Winter Park and Maitland. Then it branches roughly into four geographic groupings, north, south, east and west. Entries in each of the categories are alphabetical: not arranged in the order of importance. The judgments are yours to make.

Most public facilities these days are constructed to accommodate wheelchairs. Special arrangements, if any, are mentioned in the text of each location. For specifics, or if there is any doubt, you can write or telephone before visiting. Mailing address and telephone number of each destination are listed.

The book concludes with a handy topical cross reference.

Have a happy trip.

Orlando Is . . .

Come with us now on a quick tour of Orlando, from the time when it was a campground for U.S. soldiers during the Second Seminole War (1835–1842) to its status today as the vacation capital of the world.

* One of those early-day soldiers was Orlando Reeves, killed by the Indians while on night sentry duty; and if you think that's how Orlando got its name, you're right. According to one legend, anyway.

* Another legend attributes the naming of the city to a wealthy plantation owner named Orlando Rees.

* Aaron Jernigan set up a trading post here in the late 1840s, a post office was established in 1850 near Fort Gatlin, a courthouse opened in 1863 under the Confederate flag, and Orlando was incorporated in 1875.

* Orlando consisted of one square mile of land and 85 citizens in 1875.

* Orlando, the Orange County seat, sprawls for 43 square miles today and bulges with well over 130,000 residents.

* Population of metropolitan Orlando is about 750,000 in an area that also boasts more than 2,000 lakes and canals.

* Citrus, plus construction of a railroad to Sanford in 1885, created Orlando's first boom.

* The Great Freeze of 1895 halted the boom, to be replaced in the 1920s by a land boom.

* During the Depression years Orlando slept quietly as a nice little orange grove town.

* Orlando Air Base was a vital military facility during World War II, and the area furnished its share of wartime heroes.

* Between 1950 and 1960 the Orlando area population jumped 124 percent. Much of the increase was due (in addition to a pleasant climate) to the birth of John F. Kennedy Space

Orange Avenue in downtown Orlando got a facelift in 1984. Trees, benches, new lights, widened sidewalks and new street surface were first steps of multi-million-dollar Streetscape project. Photo by George Skene.

Center 50 miles to the east at Cape Canaveral, followed by a number of related industries in electronics, engineering and defense manufacturing, including the huge Martin Marietta Corporation's Orlando Division.

* McCoy Air Force (SAC) Base was also in full bloom in the 1950s.

* The Naval Training Center at Orlando opened in 1968.

* Walt Disney World opened in 1971, created a building boom, and spawned a number of other major tourist attractions.

* In 1974 McCoy AFB deactivated, and turned over the property for expansion and development of Orlando International Airport.

* City of Orlando owns the modern Mayor Bob Carr Performing Arts Centre, and Orlando Stadium where the nationally televised Florida Citrus Bowl NCAA Football Classic is played in December.

* Orlando has two major professional golf tournaments each year: Arnold Palmer's Bay Hill Classic and the PGA Team Championship at Disney World.

* Metro Orlando is the home of University of Central Florida, Rollins College, Valencia Community College (East and West), and Seminole Community College.

* Orlando has one of the finest public library systems in the Southeast.

* Disney World now outranks the Eiffel Tower as the world's most popular tourist attraction.

* Orlando is the home of the renowned Florida Symphony Orchestra, and one of the state's most progressive daily newspapers, *The Orlando Sentinel.*

* Metro Orlando has more than 300 houses of worship, 17 hospitals, 30 golf courses, close to 35,000 hotel and motel rooms, and the third best drinking water in the country (according to a recent survey).

* Orlando's Ben White Raceway is one of the finest winter training facilities (November through May) for trotters and pacers in the World.

* The emergence in 1974—and continuing expansion—of Church Street Station, a two-city-block entertainment complex

centered around the old railroad depot and topped by Rosie O'Grady's Goodtime Emporium, has triggered a refurbishing of downtown Orlando and a high-rise office building boom.
* Orlando is a warm blend of citrus groves and tourism, a mixed bag of industry, agriculture and finance, an easy atmosphere wrapped in sweet air.

And now the details. All aboard, folks.

When Driving in Florida . . .

* You're permitted to turn right through a red traffic light—but only after coming to a full stop and yielding to pedestrian and cross traffic.

* Under only one condition are you permitted to make a left turn on a red light: when you've already committed yourself to the middle of an intersection on a green light and are waiting for the flow of on-coming traffic to cease. If you're out there in no-man's land when the light turns red, you can make your left turn. Exercise caution because you're at the courteous mercy of drivers who are ready to proceed on a green light.

* Come to a full stop at a flashing red traffic signal. Then proceed with caution.

* You can pass another vehicle on the right—as long as you do not drive on the shoulder of the road.

* If you're involved in an accident resulting in death, injury or at least $50 property damage, you must notify local police or the highway patrol.

* If convicted of a moving traffic violation, the conviction is forwarded to your home state.

Beal-Maltbie Shell Museum

Odd, isn't it, that one of the world's biggest and finest shell collections should be housed in an inland city of this peninsular state?

The Beal-Maltbie Shell Museum, with its treasures of the tides from the farthest corners of the earth, is located just inside the entrance to the Rollins College campus in Winter Park. In this museum are about two million shells representing close to 100,000 species, displayed in a room without windows to protect them from the sun.

The collection was begun in 1888 by Dr. James H. Beal of Merritt Island (Florida). He collected his first shells in Key West, continuing his search wherever he could personally discover them, and purchasing them from myriad sources in this country and internationally. His goal was to establish an aesthetic and educational exhibit for the American public.

He came up with the sacred shell of the Hindus; shells created by animals which secrete a deadly poison; shells which the Chinese and Filipinos used as a substitute for window glass; shells worn by Polynesians as badges of rank; shells which imbed in wood; shells used for money and baking dishes; and, of course, the shell used to start this collection.

The museum list is practically endless. Just outside the entrance is a 300-pound shell serving as a drain for the drinking fountain.

Four years before Dr. Beal's death in 1945, Dr. Birdsay L. Maltbie endowed Rollins College with the funds to build a Mediterranean style building (in keeping with the general architectural scheme of the atmospheric campus), specifically to house and exhibit the shell collection of his lifelong friend. Many other private collections have since been added at the museum.

Dr. Maltbie's gift to the state's oldest co-educational college was a direct tribute to Dr. Beal, with the proviso that it would be open to the public. And so it is, Monday through Friday from 10 a.m. to 5 p.m. The museum is closed on weekends, and usually the last two weeks in August and for two weeks during the Christmas holidays. Admission price is $1 for adults, 50 cents for those 6 to 12. Children under 6 admitted free. Shell-type gifts are available for purchase.

The Way to Go: Take the Fairbanks Avenue exit from Interstate 4 (three miles north of downtown Orlando). Proceed east for three miles on Fairbanks to Park Avenue (seventh stoplight from the interstate). Turn right on Park, drive one short block and turn left onto the campus. If you're in Orlando and prefer to stay off the interstate, travel north on Mills Avenue (Mills becomes Orlando Avenue when it crosses into Winter Park), turn right at Route 426 East (Orange Avenue) and drive another mile to the college. The shell museum is across the first campus street from Sandspur (soccer) Field.

Mayor Carl T. Langford Park

No need to go tromping through forest and swamp, risking snakebite and chigger itch, for a close look at a miniature jungle. Almost within walking distance of downtown Orlando there's a half-mile stretch of boardwalk—enlivened by a short, bouncy suspension bridge—that needles through 17.3 leafy acres to give visitors a front-row view of untampered, subtropical nature.

This is Mayor Carl T. Langford Park, carved out and cared for by the Orlando Parks and Recreation Department. Nature, conservation and education are its themes. Nothing exotic has been added. Except for construction of the boardwalk, it's as if man had never been here.

The environment is sensitive. It can get marshy, and there are the inevitable sightings of snakes, thus the boardwalk is a necessity. In addition, there is a half-mile of crushed coquina rock trail that twists adventurously, back where the underbrush has been permitted to climb and crowd the visitor and create a humidity factor. By design, strollers come upon three decisively different atmospheres: cool but humid, cool shade, and sun.

There are about 70 strategically placed rustic signs that explain about the trickle of Fern Creek and erosion, and that identify trees and birds and anything else the visitor might sight along the way. After a walk through, and reading the signs, even children can get a grasp of how man and the environment are dependent upon each other for survival—Florida style. If lucky, you'll catch glimpses of the rabbits, squirrels and raccoons that live in the middle of the park.

This is not one of those places where caretakers holler at kids if they climb all over the big sign out front. In fact, the sign, constructed of heavy, staggered beams, is meant to be climbed and romped about on. Playground equipment and picnic areas are also located on the grounds.

Orlando Parks and Recreation Department built this facility with wheelchair traffic in mind. Open from 6 a.m. to one hour after sunset. No admission charge.

The Way to Go: East from downtown Orlando on Central Boulevard. From Orange Avenue, which slices the heart of downtown, the distance is only 15 short blocks. Hampton Avenue marks the eastern boundary of the park.

Orlando Science Center

You'll have to excuse some hometown folks if they still call this award-winning facility by its old name, the John Young Science Center.

John Young. The name should be as familiar to newcomers as the man is to oldtime Orlandoans. John Young: United States astronaut, spacecraft commander of both Apollo 16 and the first space shuttle, the man who once held the record for having lived more hours in space than anyone in the history of humankind.

John Young spent his early years in Orlando, and attended now defunct Orlando High School before taking off into the world of higher learning at Georgia Tech and ending—well, who knows just how high into space his education will conclude? He has been toasted and saluted many times in his hometown, with probably the most distinguished honor bestowed in the late 1970s when the name of Central Florida Museum was changed to John Young Museum & Planetarium.

That made a lot of people happy. Then in 1983, the science center came into a lot of money—but there was a catch. And that made a lot of people unhappy.

According to the will of an Orlando man who died that year, the center would receive a six-figure portion of his estate if the facility would be renamed Orlando Science Center. Apparently the deceased's family and friends had no inkling of why his gift carried the name-change clause, but the will was clear and ironbound.

Thus, the science center's board of directors was faced with a paradox of major controversial proportions. The money was direly needed for improvements. No one argued that point. Yet, was the monetary sum worth the rather shamefaced action of removing the name of an authentic hometown hero?

The community and news media leaped into the controversy. Everyone, it seemed, has his say. Even John Young himself. And when he raised no howl, magnanimously offering to go along with whatever was beneficial for the community, the board, with admitted reluctance, decided to accept the money and change the name.

As any visitor to the museum can plainly observe, the money was put to excellent use. and the astronaut's name is still highly visible, both in his continued contributions to the space program, and on one of Orlando's vital thoroughfares, the John Young Parkway.

The museum, a non-profit institution supported by the public, is set in Loch Haven Park, a 10-minute drive from downtown Orlando. Although it's not the biggest museum in the southeast, it is one of the more interesting in this part of the country, a favorite stomping grounds for inquisitive minds of all ages, and it's equipped for wheelchair patronage.

Even if you get no farther than the museum sales shop just inside the entrance, you can regard your visit worthwhile. The display of science-related souvenirs and gifts—space medallions, minerals, jewelry, instruments, books, etc.—is tasteful, offbeat, and the prices reasonable.

But you really must go into the museum proper. There is a Discovery Room with dozens of permanent and temporary exhibits. The Transparent Anatomical Manikin, 5 feet, 8 inches (1.6 meters) of clear plastic, is the only one of its kind in Florida. The systems of the human body are visible and as each lights up, TAM—that's the model's nickname—describes the functions. All kinds of excitement in the Discovery Room: see your own heartbeat, a glass-enclosed beehive in natural surroundings, live Florida-type reptiles and other amphibians, and so on.

Throughout the year the museum offers specials like family lectures, movies and demonstrations, and there are annual pet fairs and kite days. These events are announced to museum members in special bulletins, and in the news media, but you can check them out or obtain membership information and other specifics by writing Orlando Science Center, Loch Haven Park, Orlando, FL 32803. Telephone: (305) 896-7151.

The museum opens at 9 a.m., Monday through Friday; and at noon on Saturday and Sunday. It closes at 5 p.m. Monday through Thursday; at 9 p.m. on Friday and Saturday; and at 5 p.m. on Sunday. Regular admissions for non-members: $1.75 for adults, $1.25 for those under the age of 18, and $1.25 for senior citizens. The starting age for senior citizens here is 55.

The multi-media space shows in the planetarium every day of the week are the most popular presentations. The tools are a highly advanced star projector, motion picture footage and other visuals, and a 40-foot domed screen—and the result is spectacular. Shows are programmed Monday through Thursday at 2:30 p.m.; Friday at 2:30 and 8 p.m.; Saturday and Sunday at 2 and 3:30 p.m. They change about every two and a half months.

Inaugurated in 1980 and rocketing in popularity are the planetarium's weekend cosmic musical concerts set to special effects. It's best to check for times and titles, and to get a rundown on all the nocturnal productions and, in fact, on all the new presentations available and in the works. The center, in effect, reflects the fast-moving world.

One of the standard highlights, however, is the Carolyn Wine Observatory (named for an Orlando businesswoman and civic activist), where you peek in on the outer space community through a 32 centimeter (12½ inch) reflector and other telescopes. The practice has been to open the "Sky Watch" observatory at 9 p.m. on Fridays on clear nights, but here again you're advised to call ahead. No admission fee.

Call Orlando Science Center what you will, but it's an exciting place to visit in any case.

The Way to Go: Take the Loch Haven Park-Princeton Street exit off Interstate 4. Drive east on Princeton for less than a mile, then turn left onto the spacious brick parking lot. If you're coming from SR 50 (Colonial Drive), wheel north on Mills Avenue (17-92), and turn left on Rollins Street at the fifth traffic light (before crossing the Andrews Causeway). Take the second driveway to the left to the museum.

Leu Gardens

Camellias and azaleas help celebrate the new year with quiet brilliance. The 400 bushes in the formal rose garden, along with a variety of spring-flowering trees, take a well-deserved bow from April through June. Summer's center stage belongs to the loyal and lovely annuals. Then, September through December, orchids render the ultimate of their spectacular color.

That's the calendar story of Leu Gardens, a 55-acre botanical showplace in the middle of Orlando, open to the public every day except Christmas.

The late Harry P. Leu, an Orlando businessman, lived on this tract with his family until 1961 when he decided to turn it over to the City of Orlando—with the proviso that the plants he had collected on expeditions around the world be incorporated into a public garden. The city now maintains the property at an annual maintenance and expansion budget of $300,000.

Mr. Leu's gift to the city included a two-story, eight-room house, built in 1898 and currently under restoration by the Orange County Historical Society as an exhibition of early Florida lifestyle.

Leu Gardens was originally designed as a drive-through facility. Today, most of the driveways are pathways. Other visitor foot trails have been added, providing a complete walk-through attraction with wheelchair access. A leisurely stroll through the garden takes about an hour and a half.

There are a number of resting places for visitors along the way. Topping the list are the benches beneath a vine-covered trellis with a neat view along the dogwood-lined mall to the gazebo. The handsome gazebo provides shelter from the sun and those clockwork summertime rains. It's a place of relaxation, of meditation.

The conservatory near the garden entrance has a small waterfall, lush green tropical setting, and generous sprays of orchids. One of the most popular picture-snapping stops is the unique Floral Clock, planted and fashioned on a graceful slant of ground. There are sculptures, fountains, footbridges over a stream, serene green everywhere, and flashing colors, archways of oaks, citrus trees, an avenue of camphor trees, a Memorial Garden with a view of Lake Rowena, and a garden featuring plants indigenous to Central Florida. Don't miss that magnificent red cedar near the office.

Well, just be sure to pick up a detailed map of the entire layout so you don't miss anything. If you do overlook anything at all, this tender trap of nature merits revisiting—again and again, season after season. Leu Gardens opens every day at 9 a.m. and closes at 5 p.m. There's an admission charge of 50 cents per person. Children under 12 admitted free. No concessions, no gift shop. Telephone (305) 894-6021 for the latest news on blooms.

Orlando is known as The City Beautiful. Leu Gardens is one of the reasons.

The Way to Go: Take the Loch Haven-Princeton exit from Interstate 4. Princeton dead-ends into Route 17-92 (Mills Avenue). Turn right, then turn left at the first traffic light on Nebraska Avenue. You can see Leu Gardens on your left as you approach the yellow blinker signal at Forest Avenue, but you'll have to turn left onto Forest to make the swing into the park. Or drive north on Mills from Colonial Drive (SR 50), and continue to Virginia Drive (third traffic light from Colonial). Turn right, follow the signs, and turn left immediately after the yellow blinker.

Loch Haven
Art Center

Noted for its quality and variety of art exhibits for two decades, the Loch Haven Art Center attained a rank of distinction in September of 1979 with the opening of the permanent Pre-Columbian Gallery.

The 250 pieces of the Pre-Columbian collection—one of the finest in Southeastern United States—represent 50 different styles extracted from Mexico, Peru, Guatemala, Columbia, Costa Rica and Panama, dating from 1200 B.C. to 1500 A.D.

The Collection originated with the donation of the private collection of Howard Campbell in 1972, and since then it has been supplemented by donations from other private collectors and by persons interested in purchasing pieces for the art center. All the amassing and utilization of these works have remained faithful to Mr. Campbell's original desire to afford the public an opportunity to view and appreciate Pre-Columbian civilizations and the unique aesthetic strains of their art.

The Pre-Columbian educational alcove seems more a tasteful entertainment: giant map with flashing lights, bilingual tapes and first-class slide-tape programs. An enlarged reproduction of a Mayan Temple lithograph created by Frederick Catherwood occupies a full wall, measuring about 15 feet wide and 10 feet high. The scene depicts the discovery of a small pyramid in the center of the Mayan town Tulum which was built on a cliff overlooking the Caribbean on the eastern coast of the Yucatan Peninsula of Mexico.

Art purists have expressed appreciation for the unstinting research by art center personnel in bringing the most authentic archeological information to its majestic Pre-Columbian presentation.

Loch Haven Art Center, a non-profit educational institution, began as Orlando Art Association, Inc., in 1926. The group moved into its first building in Loch Haven Park in 1960, changed its name in 1968, and opened its present building the following year. Governed by an executive committee and board of trustees, the art center was one of the first museums in the country to receive professional accreditation by the American Association of Museums, and has been bestowed many community service awards.

Year-round classes in painting, drawing, sculpture, etching, stained glass, block printing and photography, taught by professionals, are offered for adults and children. Visiting artists also set up workshops and present lectures. Each year 15,000 students take part in art enrichment programs.

Loch Haven Art Center's changing exhibits are always interesting, covering a broad range of periods, styles and media, obtained from internationally known museums and private collections. One of the most popular recently was the exhibition of life-size realistic figures by Florida sculptor Duane Hanson, who developed the use of polymer resin and fiber in his art. Following timely exposure in the *Orlando Sentinel Star,* thousands of Central Floridians and visitors lined up on the grounds to see the show.

Loch Haven Park was donated to the City of Orlando by the Dr. Phillips Foundation, and also serves as the setting for the Edyth Bush Theater, Orlando Science Center, Orange County Historical Museum, Garden Club and Junior Achievement. The art center, which is funded by the city, the county, membership dues and by numerous public and private sources, occupies the northeast corner of the pretty property, along Mills Avenue and Rollins Street.

Except for certain exhibits, there is no admission charge to Loch Haven Art Center. Hours: 10 a.m. to 5 p.m., Tuesday through Friday; noon to 5 p.m. on Saturday; and 2 p.m. to 5 p.m. on Sunday. Closed on Monday and certain holidays. There's a free-wheeling surface for wheelchairs inside the center, and a runway at the entrance.

Mailing address: Loch Haven Art Center, Inc., 2416 N. Mills Ave., Orlando, FL 32803. Telephone: (305) 896-4231.

The Way to Go: Take the Loch Haven Park-Princeton Street exit off Interstate 4. Drive east on Princeton for less than a mile, then turn left onto the spacious brick parking lot. If you're traveling from SR 50 (Colonial Drive), come north on Mills Avenue (US 17-92). You can turn left on Princeton, but it's easier to make the left at the traffic signal on Rollins Street (fifth traffic light from Colonial).

Maitland
Art Center

"Let your thoughts rest here awhile in beauty and in love."

These deep, soft words, carved on the premises in stone, set the tone for a poetic experience: a visit to Maitland Art Center, a museum that overshadows its exhibitions. Don't pass up a chance to come and feel its throbbing pulse.

The art center, originally named the Research Center, was built in 1937 by Jules Andre Smith and Mrs. Mary Curtis Bok Zimbalist, a classic collaboration of artist and patron. Smith's motive: create a commune for avant garde artists, a retreat where they could work in peace (and dwell with their families) free of the pressures to earn a living.

Who was this man Smith who bequeathed the art world and the Orlando area so remarkable a legacy? Yes, he's gone now; died in 1959 at the age of 78. Jules Andre Smith was more than a painter; he was an architect, etcher, sculptor, stage designer, humanitarian, author, and a dreamer who carved his dreams into reality. A graduate of Cornell University, he worked two years as a draftsman and designer for an architectural firm in New York, but favorable response to his spare time paintings and etchings was all the stimulus he needed to change careers.

Smith traveled widely overseas, and was influenced by the European artists' revolt from tradition. He produced wild and wonderful work, but after awhile abandoned this style. Today we can examine his precise etchings and see the stunning contrast to some of his earlier experiments in pointillism, and forms rubbed on glass with his fingers and printed on paper. Smith was an artist of compassion, uncommon versatility, integrity and skill.

Serving as a first lieutenant in an Army engineers camouflage company during World War I, Smith was assigned to battlefronts in France and Germany where he sketched action scenes of America's involvement; and he was commissioned by General William H. Black to design the Distinguished Service Cross.

Returning to civilian life, Smith published 100 of his war front drawings in *In France with the American Expeditionary Forces,* a book hailed by critics.

Smith had survived the war, but he really can't be regarded as one of the lucky ones. In officers' training school he had sustained a leg injury that did not heal properly, and in 1924 suffered a massive embolism, forcing surgeons to amputate the leg above the knee. He endured unbelievable suffering. In later years he had to give up etchings because of failing eyesight.

At the age of 55, on a drive through Florida from his home and studio at Stony Creek, Connecticut, Smith discovered the little Orange County town of Maitland, not far from Orlando.

His Research Studio, now the Maitland Art Center, is composed of walled compounds on both sides of brick-paved Packwood Avenue. The simple architecture of the cement buildings is enriched by more than 200 ornamental carvings. Smith, noteworthily, was one of the first artists to carve in wet cement—as opposed to casting in molds. His whimsical sense of experimentation is evident at the center in combinations of Christian and Buddhist iconography, Mayan motifs, Aztec birds and figures, abstract panels and figurative sculptures. Fancy gates and screens of wrought iron grace the buildings.

The Garden Chapel on the south side of Packwood was added in 1942, and dedicated to the artist's mother who nursed him through his illness. The chapel is now maintained by the City of Maitland, and is the site of many wedding ceremonies.

The chapel entry is a lavishly ornamented covered narthex, or porch, while the chapel itself is open to the sky. Wall carvings portray the life of Jesus Christ. There is a trellised walkway, adorned with pagan gods. There's a meeting room with a fireplace and colorful murals. Behind the chapel is a small room, used by Smith as a gallery for his painted cement abstract panels. Astoundingly, the artist performed just about all the construction work himself, or directed competent artisans when he could find them.

He was an artist who never let color or creed interfere with his promulgation of art or equal lifestyles. He designed the Black New Hope Church in Winter Park, long before black awareness became fashionable, executed murals for a black church in nearby Eatonville, and in one of the most conspicuous walls in his own chapel he imbedded a carved-cement relief of a Black Madonna and Child by Wilma Wolfs.

In the main building of the bigger compound on the opposite side of the road is a gallery which houses a permanent collection and monthly rotating exhibits. From here you can step into a peaceful garden and courtyard, surrounded by apartments and studios, originally designed for visiting artists and their families and now utilized as classrooms.

Smith offered fellowships at his Research Studio from November 1 to May 1 each year to American artists, selected for their individuality and promise. Among those who wintered with Smith were Hal McIntosh, Bill Orr, Charles Prendergrast, Boris Margo, Maxwell Parrish, Doris Lee and Ralston Crawford.

Today, the only artists-in-residence are Jim Cook, a potter, and his wife Terri, a graphics artist.

Maitland Art Center is open from 10 a.m. to 4 p.m., Tuesday through Friday; and from 1 p.m. to 4 p.m. on Saturday and Sunday. Closed on Monday. No admission charge. Mailing address: Maitland Art Center, 231 W. Packwood Avenue, Maitland, FL 32751. Telephone (305) 645-2181.

Maitland Art Center, taken as the creative effort of one man, is one of the country's most noble examples of original architecture and art.

The Way to Go: Take the Maitland Avenue exit (Route 426-A) off Interstate 4. Travel east about two miles to Maitland Avenue. Turn right. This is also Route 427 South. Drive not quite a mile and turn right at Packwood Avenue. You're 30 seconds away from your destination. Or drive north from SR 50 (Colonial Drive) on Mills Avenue (17-92) to Maitland. It's about five miles from Colonial to Packwood Avenue. Turn left, go over railroad tracks and drive another block.

"Feeding the Flamingos," by Louis Tiffany is part of the permanent exhibition at the Morse Gallery of Art. Reproduced by permission of Doubleday & Company.

Morse
Gallery of Art

Small, clubby, very tasteful, and the greatest collection of Tiffany glass and jewelry in the world—that's the Morse Gallery of Art in downtown Winter Park.

Lovers of exquisite artistry will love it, and for admirers of the work of the late Louis Comfort Tiffany, a visit here is imperative. Included are most of the pieces the artist himself labeled as his best—plus the work of Tiffany contemporaries and other artists who were influenced by the master. The collection is owned by Hugh and Jeannette Genius McKean.

Hugh McKean now serves as director of the gallery. As a young man he was one of several artists from around the country invited to live and work at the fabled Tiffany estate, Laurelton Hall, in Long Island. Tiffany was already an old man at the time, and McKean only met him briefly, but he's carried on a lifelong affair with the Tiffany art.

McKean's own career as an artist was sidetracked by academics. Although he continued to paint—and still does—he became an art professor, and later president and chancellor of Rollins College in Winter Park. McKean and his wife went to the New York estate a number of years ago and purchased a bulk of the Tiffany work, at a time when Tiffany popularity had tarnished. The McKeans stepped in and virtually saved much of the art before a demolition crew's bulldozer could sweep it into oblivion (following a fire at the estate). Today their collection, started with pieces Mrs. McKean inherited from her parents, is truly priceless.

McKean furnishes a neat history of the Tiffany art, a personalized profile of the artist, and a well-written commentary of his own involvement with both, in a big gorgeously-illustrated book (it really is gorgeous) titled *The 'Lost' Treasures of Louis Tiffany,* published in late 1980 by Doubleday.

The Tiffany exhibitions at the gallery are limited in size at any one time, and change often, and the McKeans receive an unending flow of requests for pieces to exhibit in other galleries in Florida and elsewhere, but anything one gets to inspect here—glass, leaded glass windows, pottery, jewelry, metal wares, fancy goods, etc.—make a visit priceless.

The gallery is open Tuesday through Saturday from 9:30 a.m. to 4 p.m., and Sunday from 1 to 4 p.m. Small admission charge. Mailing address: Morse Gallery of Art, 151 E. Welbourne Avenue, Winter Park, FL 32789. Telephone: (305) 645-5311.

The Way to Go: Take the Fairbanks exit from Interstate 4 (three miles north of downtown Orlando). Drive east for three miles on Fairbanks to Park Avenue. Turn left on Park; then right three blocks later on Welbourne. Morse Gallery of Art is located halfway down the short block on the left.

Navy World

On the premise that everybody loves a parade, the Naval Training Center in Orlando opens its gates every Friday morning and invites the public to sit in on recruit graduation.

Each week approximately 600 enlisted men and women, who have come through boot training, pass-in-review. It's a colorful ritual, and a highly emotional time as the Navy Band Orlando, the famous Bluejacket Chorus, the 50-state flag team, and two precision drill teams combine to give graduates a sendoff as they head out to naval careers in the U.S. and around the world.

By all means bring a camera to the exercises.

The Naval Training Center, one of the biggest and most modern facilities of its kind in the world, was commissioned in 1968. Recruit training is just part of the action. The complex comprises 15,000 military and civilian personnel who make up 25 various commands and activities, from boot camp to highly specialized training for both enlisted and officer Navy men and women.

The first class of 393 men graduated from Orlando's Recruit Training Command on December 12, 1968; and the first class with women in the ranks passed-in-review five years later. All enlisted females take their initial training here. The other two

Navy World, where each week approximately 600 enlisted men and women graduate from the Naval Training Center and pass-in-review in a colorful parade.

boot camps for enlisted men are located at Great Lakes, Illinois, and San Diego, California.

To date, more than 300,000 men and women recruits have graduated from the Orlando facility. Graduation ceremonies start at 9:45 a.m., and last about an hour. No admission charge. Telephone: (305) 646-4474.

The Way to Go: Driving east on Interstate 4, or north on Magnolia Avenue (a one-way street out of downtown Orlando), turn off on E. Colonial Drive (SR 50). Travel east on Colonial for ten blocks, then turn left (north) at the busy Mills Avenue intersection. Continue along Mills until reaching Virginia Drive (three stoplights from Colonial), turn right and follow signs. Entrance to the Recruit Training Command is on General Rees Road, a left turn just short of Navy World's main gate.

Orange County Historical Museum

Now that you're in Orlando, the vacation capital of the world, wouldn't it be interesting to see what it looked like when the Orange County seat was a one-horse town?

Actually, as Jean Yothers, director of the Orange County Historical Museum, prefers to humorously point out, Orlando was never a one-horse town—and she has a mid-19th century photograph to prove it. Orlando was a two-horse town!

As you might guess, this museum is a fun place to visit. Serving as a repository for Orange County's past, it is overflowing with old photos of homes, street scenes and personalities, nostalgic newspapers, badges, buttons, banners, flags, furniture, clothing, farm tools, toys, a hitching post and a gaslight fountain, a Victorian parlor, a 1,500-pound bell, an 1883 Steinway piano and an 1870s Everette piano, a cracker whip, ancient telephones, myriad antiques, a railway exhibit, archeological findings, surprises and interesting tidbits at every turn to make you smile or stir your imagination or memory; countless carryovers from a slice of Florida that was primarily a wilderness of military trails, forts, cattle ranches, citrus groves and turpentine stills.

The museum itself dates back to 1942 when a few women set up a pioneer kitchen in Orlando's old red-brick courthouse as part of a county-wide observance of a Century of Progress. The kitchen remained, a museum evolved, and in 1976 moved to a permanent home in Loch Haven Park, a 10-minute drive from downtown. The museum is funded by the county, and run by the Orange County Historical Society, Inc. This membership society has also assumed fund-raising responsibility for expansion. The museum keeps getting bigger.

Standing about are a number of lifesized figures in period clothing, an especially effective device in the popular old timey country store exhibit. There are replicas of Fort Gatlin, which protected pioneers from Indian attacks, and the original Pine Castle, a neighboring community.

There are also replicas of Billy the Swan, once identified as the Tyrant of Lake Lucerne, and of proud Percy, a member of the renowned peacock pack along Genius Drive in Winter Park. Moonshine stills played a part in Orange County's past, too, although that chunk of nostalgia, an honest-to-gosh still, has been taken off the exhibit line.

Orange County Historical Museum, sharing a lobby with the Orlando Science Center, is a memory walk where you can trace the establishment and rise of the county's lifestyle, from back in the days when the county was named Mosquito, from the bleak days of the Seminole Wars, through the citrus blossoming, the Big Freeze of 1894, the land boom of the 1920s, and on to the present. And let's not forget the 1960s real estate boom ignited by the coming of Walt Disney World. There is also a complete hot-type printing exhibit, courtesy of *The Orlando Sentinel.*

The museum is closed on Monday. Other weekday hours are from 10 a.m. to 4 p.m. The Saturday and Sunday hours are 2 to 5 p.m. Admission is free. Arrangements can be quickly made for walking tours in English, Spanish and French. A Braille guidebook is available, and there are facilities for the disabled.

Guided group tours should be arranged in advance: Orange County Historical Museum, 812 Rollins St., Orlando, FL 32803.

You've heard of Florida's sleepy orange grove towns. That's what Orlando was. And, as Orlando slept, so did Orange County. And it wasn't so long ago.

The Way to Go: Take the Loch Haven Park exit off Interstate 4 (Princeton Street), and drive east for just over a half-mile, then turn left into the park on the huge, brick-paved parking lot. Or, if you're coming from Colonial Drive (SR 50), drive north on Mills Avenue (17-92). Turn left at Rollins Street (fifth stoplight from Colonial), then make another left at the second driveway.

Park Avenue

In Central Florida, Park Avenue means downtown Winter Park.

The downtown strip of this street stretches arrestingly for 10 blocks—from the edge of Rollins College on the south to St. Margaret Mary School on the north—much of the street bordered on the westside by a neat, tree-filled park.

For anyone with selective eating, buying and browsing in mind, Park Avenue is a bonanza. It has ordinary shops, and it has quaint, European-styled shops in hidden gardens. It has exclusive stores for men and women; offices for brokers, attorneys and architects; banks; a grocery store and a liquor store; a modern fully-stocked book shop; antiques; art galleries and studios; a dime store; a unique hotel; a bakery; pharmacies; city hall; a church.

For the hungry and the thirsty, Park Avenue has everything from snacks and soup and health food to La Belle Verriere, one of Central Florida's quality restaurants. At Brandywine's Deli & Restaurant on the north end of the strip you can eat in the sun if you prefer.

The fairly new St. Margaret Mary Church at the Canton intersection crowns Park Avenue with an aesthetic and spiritual dimension. The interior of the church is tastefully modern with pews fanned out from the clean lines of the altar. The atmosphere is restful and inspirational. Visitors welcomed. Three other nearby churches, while not on Park Avenue itself, should not be missed. From St. Margaret Mary's, drive east on Canton for a block to Interlachen Avenue. Canton dead-ends here. Turn right on Interlachen and drive a block to Winter Park Methodist Church. It occupies the block between Lincoln and Morse Boulevard. Continue south on Intelachen for two blocks to First Congregational United Church of Christ; then another block south to All Saints' Episcopal Church.

All three of these beautiful churches are open during the day for prayer and meditation, although visitors to All Saints are asked to check in first at the office behind the church, across the street from the parking lot of the Langford Resort Hotel.

By no elongation of imagination can Park Avenue be depicted as a shopping mall. There is no directory. There is no noticeable, continuing architectural theme. Each place of business, standing shoulder to shoulder, is characteristic only unto itself. While here, don't overlook the several short streets off Park.

Most shops close on Sunday, and few stay open beyond 5:30 p.m. on the other six nights. Once upon a time half the stores closed down in the summer months, but no more.

Park Avenue, home of the gigantic Sidewalk Art Festival each spring, is a narrow, slow-moving street with two-hour-limit parking on both sides. Parking can be a problem on Saturdays and during rush seasons, but the city provides spacious lots for this purpose a short distance to the west, just beyond the Amtrak line.

And there's always that shaded park across the street, forever beckoning leg-weary meanderers.

For dates of the art festival, special events and general information, contact Winter Park Chamber of Commerce, P.O. Box 280, Winter Park, FL 32790. Telephone: (305) 644-8281. The chamber building is located next to the post office on New York Avenue, the parallel block to the west of Park Avenue.

The Way to Go: Take the Fairbanks Avenue exit from Interstate 4 (three miles north of downtown Orlando). Drive east for three miles on Fairbanks to Park Avenue (it's the seventh stoplight from the interstate). Turn left.

Polasek
Foundation

Albin Polasek, internationally known sculptor and painter, spent the last 16 years of his life in Winter Park. He came here in 1949 after retiring as head of the Department of Sculpture at Chicago Art Institute, and designed and built a museum-like studio-home on a three-acre estate bordered by Lake Osceola.

Shortly after its completion, he suffered a partially paralyzing stroke and was confined to a wheelchair. But he did not consider himself a prisoner of that wheelchair. He vigorously pursued his art, almost forgetting that he had the use of only his right arm, and continued to produce stunningly impressive works.

Polasek died in 1965 at the age of 86. His widow Emily still lives in their apartment in the home, but the home is now in a private foundation and open to the public. Acceding to the artist's wishes there is no admission charge. An immigrant from Frenstadt, Moravia (now Czechoslovakia), Polasek was a self-taught artist who came up the hard way and he wanted his art to be easily accessible to the American people.

Yet, perhaps because Mrs. Polasek closes the home in the summer, the Polasek Foundation is one of the least known, least visited museums in Central Florida. Certainly, though, it is one of the most engaging. The home, galleries and graceful grounds are scattered with eye-catchers, all the pieces the artist referred to as his "children." Found here among the original presentations are many replicas of pieces which brought him world acclaim.

Museum hours, October through June: 10 a.m. to noon and 1 p.m. to 4 p.m., Wednesday through Saturday; and 1 p.m. to 4 p.m. on Sunday. Closed Monday and Tuesday. Mailing address: Polasek Foundation, 633 Osceola Avenue, Winter Park, FL 32789. Telephone: (305) 647-6294.

Among the exhibits are "The Sower" (a second casting of the original at Chicago Art Institute and a flawless rendition of the human anatomy); the excitingly brutal "Primeval Struggle," man and wolf; a man carving himself and his destiny; "Girl with Goose;" and an unusual "Emily" fountain in the courtyard depicting the widow holding a harp with strings of trickling water spilling into a reflecting pool at her feet.

Found in the carvings is a Christmas creche Polasek created at the age of 14. Paintings, of course, many of them religious, adorn the galleries and chapel. Also in the chapel are crayon drawings of the Fourteen Stations of the Cross, and the Communion scene from the Last Supper which he executed, unbelievably, from his wheelchair. An oil re-creation of his bedroom intrigues and mystifies most beholders. There's something downright eerie about it. Depending on the angle from which it's viewed, the bed in the scene seems to assume different positions.

Little Albin Polasek at the age of 15 was a woodcarving apprentice in Vienna. Five years later he arrived in America, where two of his brothers were priests. He had little money, spoke no English, and was advised against trying to earn his way in life as an artist; but he held staunchly to his conviction that he could literally carve his own destiny. First he found work carving religious statues in stone and wood in LaCrosse, Wisconsin, then studied for a year with the great Charles Grafly. A series of prizes enabled him to study at American Academy in Rome and the Pennsylvania Academy of Fine Arts. Today, his statues stand in many places around the world, the work of a determined man who had indeed carved his own destiny.

Several years before his death as he sifted through his memories, Polasek revealed that of all the prizes he had accumulated in his artistic lifetime, the one he considered most important was the award given by the National Institute of Immigrant Welfare, bestowed upon those citizens of foreign birth who contributed most richly to American culture. He was as patriotic as he was religious. Often at night before retiring he and Emily would sing "God Bless America" together. He also played the piano and composed music. The piano, along with other personal belongings and antiques, are on display in the museum.

And the work he considered his most important? Probably the 48 pieces of ecclesiastical sculpture commissioned by St. Cecilia's Cathedral in Omaha, Nebraska. The centerpiece was a 14-foot crucifix he labeled "The Victorious Christ." The gilded original plaster model is now the centerpiece at the Polasek Foundation.

No ordinary crucifix is this. First of all, unlike so many other crucifixes, the head of the figure is lifted Heavenward: the moment of triumph for all mankind. After pouring his heart and soul into this creation for five weeks, the artist removed the arms and crated his masterpiece and shipped it to Roman Bronze in New York. A day or two later he awakened in the middle of the night and cried: "Oh, my God, the one arm is two inches shorter than the other!"

Polasek contacted the casting firm in New York with instructions to ship it back to his studio in Chicago. Anxiously he opened the crate. He measured the arms, and, yes, one was shorter. Although fellow artists doubted the sculptor could have labored on the statue for more than a month and not be aware of the disparity, he insisted the knowledge had come to him in a dream.

Now listen to another story and see if you can resist this invitation to visit Polasek Foundation.

It was a Sunday morning in Chicago in 1927, and work was not progressing on the Victorious Christ. The body nailed to the cross presented no problem, but Polasek had been unable to find a model for the face to represent the strength, intelligence, tenderness and triumph he sought.

There came a knock at his door. Ordinarily when engrossed in work he paid no attention to such disturbances. This time he opened the door unhesitatingly and looked upon the face of a male stranger. He was a stranger for only a moment. Numbed, the artist realized his prayer for a model had been answered.

The stranger spoke to him in his native Bohemian tongue, explaining what his occupation was, begging the sculptor to help him find work as he had so generously aided other immigrants. Polasek invited him into the studio. Intrigued by the man's face, he immediately began to work on the Christ head. "Yes, yes, there is much work around here for a man of your profession," Polasek said. "I hope you don't mind if I continue to work while we talk."

The sculptor worked, and they talked, and arrangements were made for the stranger to return at 8 a.m. the following day. The stranger did not return to the studio the next day. He never returned. Polasek never saw him again, never heard from him again. All the artist ever really knew about the stranger was that he said he was a carpenter.

The Way to Go: Take the Fairbanks Avenue exit from Interstate 4 (three miles north of downtown Orlando). Proceed east for three miles on Fairbanks, continuing past Rollins College. Fairbanks becomes Osceola Avenue at the next traffic light. Osceola bends almost immediately to the right. Look for the low-walled entrance to the museum almost immediately on the left.

Turkey Lake Park

All it takes is a brief visit to this acreage and you can see why the City of Orlando extended its geographic borders to claim the property for development as a public park.

The city purchased this land on Turkey Lake in the early 1970s to provide a multi-purpose outdoor recreational haven for residents and visitors, a facility that would also offer a better stage on which to study and appreciate this exceptional environment. At the same time the city lawmakers and conscientious citizenry, nervous about the pressure of the Orlando environment as applied by the swift and awesome expansion of population and property, decided that a rambling, well managed park would ease some of that stress.

The property was outside city limits at the time of purchase from private landowners. Once the proper annexation process was executed, development commenced. As you might guess, extreme care was wielded to disturb as little of the natural setting as possible. A special task force of young people was hired to help city employees, and on July 13, 1978, Turkey Lake Park opened.

Exact measure of the park: 173 land acres, 125 water acres.

First-time visitors from out of state will likely be tempted to pick an orange or tangerine from the trees in the 107 acres of citrus groves, but management requests that you stifle the urge to do so. The forbidden fruit is delicious when ripe, but it's harvested and sold by the city as a means to defray the cost of park upkeep. You can drive or walk through the groves.

Almost 60 acres are taken up by picnic and playground areas. Although the five big picnic pavilions are assigned on a reservation basis, the 15 smaller pavilions, accommodating up to 25 persons, are available to first comers. In addition there are 125 picnic tables, plenty of shade trees under which to spread a tablecloth and lunch, and 77 barbecue grills—plus 16 restrooms.

The five camping cabins, sleeping 10 persons each, are available to organized groups such as churches, synagogues, fraternal organizations, Boy and Girl Scouts, and such, by reservation only. There are 32 family campsites. Walking and hiking trails plunge through 175 acres of the park, and the special bicycle trail winds over the rolling terrain for more than three miles. Some rental bicycles are procurable during the summer season. No motorized bikes are permitted on the paths. Then there is swimming and fishing in twinkling Turkey Lake. Lifeguards patrol the beautiful, soft white sands of the beach, but note that the beach is closed from December to mid-March. For fishermen, there's a 200-foot wooden pier and a fish-cleaning area. Boats are rented in the summer at the concession stand.

Youngsters are sure to enjoy the cracker farm, where they mingle with the family of pets in the barnyard: ponies, cows, pigs, sheep, goats and rabbits, chickens of just about every variety, guinea hens, and, of course, turkeys. There's an old pitcher pump and well at the farm, too, an antique dinner bell and one of the biggest rendering kettles you might ever see.

Reservations for cabins and pavilions can be handled by mail: Turkey Lake Park, 3401 Hiawassee Road, Orlando, FL 32811. Or by telephone: (305) 299-5594. The park is open every day except Christmas from 9:30 a.m. to 5 p.m. (7 p.m. when Daylight Saving Time is in effect). There's a $1.00 admission charge for all persons age 2 and up.

Turkey Lake Park hasn't forgotten the disabled. There's a uniquely designed five-senses area for them, and Pavilion No. 4 is equipped with a loading ramp.

Turkey Lake, located at the southwest extremity of Orlando, is a free-wheeling expanse of fresh and clean greenery, religiously cared for, and with most of the general areas, including parking lots, hidden from each other by trees and foliage. Directional and explanatory rustic signs are prominent, so there's not much chance of getting lost. Sunny Sundays lure the biggest crowds, but even then it's doubtful you'll be stepping on anyone's heels. It's a big place. Probably the best time to visit is a warm winter day during the week—if you like the feeling of having the better half of the world to yourself.

The Way to Go: From Orange Avenue in downtown Orlando, drive west on Washington Street. After two miles, Washington becomes Old Winter Garden Road. Stay on this road for four miles, then turn left on Hiawasse Road (traffic signal). It's another three miles to the park entrance on the left. Or: From West Colonial Drive (SR 50), turn off on Hiawasse and it's a straight run to the park. Or: From Interstate 4, get off on Route 435 North. Travel not quite four miles and turn left on Conroy-

Windermere Road (traffic signal). Go another mile and turn right on Hiawasse, and you're just one more mile away from your destination. No matter which way you come, there are plenty of Turkey Lake signs along the way.

Winter Park

This is a nice place to visit—a nicer place to live.

Winter Park, rubbing shoulders with Orlando to the south is a quiet, conservative, most residential city of about 30,000 persons, brimming with civic atmosphere.

Visitors from the area and out of state, and from out of the country, can profitably spend at least a day here engaging in nothing but walking or driving and looking, discovering what gracious living in an inland Florida city is all about.

Visitors—even those who think they know the city—are advised to drop by the chamber of commerce office at 150 N. New York Avenue, next to the post office, and obtain a detailed, easy to read map which pinpoints the highpoints. The map costs 50 cents. Or you can obtain one by mail. Send 69 cents to Winter Park Chamber of Commerce, PO Box 280, Winter Park, FL 32790. Their telephone: (305) 644-8281. The office is open from 9 a.m. to 4 p.m., Monday through Friday; and closes weekends.

Inside Winter Park's borders are fourteen spring-fed lakes, five of which are linked by Venetian canals. Many of the homes along these shorelines are showplaces, and more than a few have been featured in national publications. Lake Virginia borders the south campus of Rollins College, an exclusive liberal arts school of high academic demands. Rollins was founded by a group of Congregational ministers in 1885, making it the first co-educational institution of higher learning in Florida.

Rollins is the cultural hub of Winter Park with its annual Bach Festival and Writers' Conference, recitals, concerts, museums, art shows, libraries, and its dramatic presentations in two theaters, featuring students and community actors. The Rollins

Tars play high-grade baseball, basketball, golf, soccer and tennis. Baseball Week in the spring attracts teams from such schools as Notre Dame, Dartmouth and Ohio State. The campus is also the scene of the invitational Tangerine Bowl Basketball Classic, and several swimming and diving championships.

Rollins rowing crews over the years have accumulated numerous important victories in this country and overseas. The crew maintains a boathouse on Lake Maitland, where rowers from northern schools come to race and train in late winter and early spring.

Lake Maitland and all the other lakes are easy to find by using the chamber of commerce map—in addition to locations of parks, schools, hospital, places of worship, a new public library, Scenic Drive, scenic boat tours, galleries, shopping areas like Park Avenue and Winter Park Mall, and Genius Drive with its rare, colorful peacock flock.

Old Winter Park, roughly from Park Avenue east to Lakemont Avenue, is overstocked with magnificent oak trees, and it's through this artistic setting that the narrow streets—many of them brick paved—unfold. Price tags on residences, apartments and condominiums in this sprawling area are as fancy as one would guess. But it costs nothing to look. Winter Park High School, Winter Park Memorial Hospital, the community center, and the newer family-oriented subdivisions are situated on the eastside of Lakemont.

The original Temple orange tree stands on residential property just off Palmer Avenue in the old section of town. Owned by noted architect James Gamble Rogers, it is probably the most pampered tree in Central Florida.

For a variety of reasons—friendly weather is naturally near the top of the list—Winter Park has long been a happy retirement ground for retired military officers and men, especially from the Air Force and Navy. Orlando Air Base was a significant post during World War II; later, a wing of the Strategic Air Command was housed at McCoy Air Force Base in Orlando. Across the southeastern border of Winter Park is Navy World, with its training command and recruit training center for men and women.

Winter Park has more than its allotment of millionaires, and men and women who have made—and are still making—their marks in business, science, art, literature, politics, whatever.

Winter Park is a snug town. Some outsiders refer to it as a smug town. Yet, for all its uniqueness, its assets, and its undeniable degree of exclusivity, Winter Park is lodged in the middle of the United States cost of living index. In short, for the average family, it's affordable. Finding your place here is something else.

The Way to Go: Take the Fairbanks Avenue exit from Interstate 4 (three miles north of downtown Orlando). Proceed east for three miles on Fairbanks to New York Avenue (sixth stoplight from the interstate). Turn left on New York, drive just beyond the next stoplight (Morse Boulevard) and look for the Winter Park Chamber of Commerce building on the right.

Blue Spring
State Park

It might not be the unanimous top choice for camping, canoeing, swimming, fishing, nature walking, picnicking, snorkeling and scuba diving in Florida, although it definitely is recommended for each of these features. What sets Blue Spring State Park aside for inclusion in this book is the presence of West Indian manatees, commonly called sea cows.

Unfortunately for many visitors, the manatees only congregate here in great numbers during the winter months, from about the middle of November to the end of March. Occasionally a stray will be sighted in summer, but it might stay only 15 minutes or so before moving along to continue its swim up or down the St. Johns River.

The manatee is one of Florida's most precious and unique residents. Originally a land mammal with four legs, it gradually returned to life in the water, its hind legs evolving into a fleshy paddle. A distant relative of the elephant, the average twelve-foot adult manatee—weighing in at about one ton—often devours one hundred pounds of aquatic plants daily.

Manatees gather in Blue Spring Run during the winter months as a matter of necessity. The waters of Blue Spring, you see, offer a year-round temperature of 72 degrees. Manatees have been known to contract pneumonia and die after extended exposure in water temperatures below 60 degrees.

Not too many years ago, the shy, sensitive manatees were common throughout the coastal regions from the Carolinas to Texas, but today they survive only in Florida, and are included in the Marine Mammal Protection Act of 1972 and the Endangered Species Act of 1973, which makes it illegal to harass, capture, hunt, or kill any marine mammal. Man, apparently, is the manatee's only enemy. Manatees have been shot and cruelly mutilated by thrill-seekers; and, when surfacing to breathe every five to eight minutes or so, they have been shamelessly injured by powerboats, sometimes intentionally. Dredging, filling and pollution also threaten their extinction, so it's easy to understand why federal and state agencies have stepped in with programs of protection, and why stiff penalties are levied on anyone caught disturbing the manatee's normal behavioral patterns.

Manatees also seek wintertime refuge in other inland waterways, especially near power generating plants, but at present Blue Spring State Park offers the only known on-shore point where people can observe the sea cows in their natural habitat. Of special interest to the disabled, the wooden observation platform extending over a portion of the clear water is easily accessible by wheelchairs.

The park, located just west of Orange City in Volusia County, is scenic, clean and tightly managed. Rules for safe scuba diving are rigorously enforced by rangers. The park is open from 8 a.m. to sunset daily throughout the year. Admission is 50 cents per person, children under six admitted free. A free lecture and slide program on manatees is presented from November 1 through March. Snacks, camping supplies, rental canoes and rowboats available. For all information, call (904) 775-6888.

48

*　*　*

Now, if you don't put in for the day at Blue Spring State Park, there's time to make two worthwhile stops when returning to Orlando on US 17-92.

First is Central Florida Zoological Park, about 11 miles south of Blue Spring, a preserve of more than 100 acres with a fine, continually-improving zoo, botanical gardens and picnic facilities. Hours: 9 to 5 p.m. every day. Admissions: $3 for adults (50 per cent discount for senior citizens); $1 for boys and girls 4–12; younger children free. Telephone: (305) 323-4450.

Your next stop is 10 miles to the south, between Sanford and Longwood. Turn right upon exiting the park and you have a stunning, panoramic view of the St. Johns River, the waterway born in the marshes and swamps west of Melbourne. It's one of the rare major rivers that flows northward. Watch carefully for the small Big Tree Park marker on the right side of the highway.

Less than a mile up the cutoff road is the home of "The Senator," the largest bald cypress in the United States. Its age is estimated between 3000 and 3500 years, making it one of the oldest trees in the country. Trunk diameter is $17\frac{1}{2}$ feet, with a circumference of 47 feet. The stately Senator, standing 126 feet tall, is an awesome sight, even at the end of an eye-filling day. No charge here. Seminole County Parks & Recreation Department closes the gates at sunset.

The Way to Go: East on Interstate 4. Get off on the second (17-92) Sanford exit, about 24 miles from downtown Orlando. Turn left on 17-92; drive through DeBary into Orange City. The big Blue Spring State Park sign over the highway is easy to sight. Turn left on W. French Avenue, travel another three miles to park entrance. Roundtrip approximately 75 miles.

Bob White Field

You like old airplanes?

Here's a neat place to spend a morning or an afternoon—or a whole day if you can't tear yourself away.

Bob White Field in Zellwood, at the northeastern rim of Orange County, has one of the longest grass airstrips in Florida—3,300 feet—and it serves as the home for at least two dozen restored, vintage aircrafts, dating from 1928. Although visitors are welcome, Bob White Field is also one of the least known places to visit for the average non-flying individual, mainly because it's bedded down in a quiet, peaceful setting well off the main highway.

In fact, you can't see the field until you drive up an uneven dirt road and break through the trees.

Bob White, owner, a native of Appleton, Wisconsin, lives on the property in a two-story house; and directs a three-man shop in one of the most active rebuilding enterprises in the country. They also manufacture steel T-Hangars, which are shelters for airplanes, usually nested tail-to-tail when set up.

Perhaps the most glamorous airship in this extremely unusual and interesting collection of tail draggers and byplanes is a Japanese Zero. Actually, it's a Canadian Mark IV Harvard, converted into a World War II fighter specifically for the movie "Tora Tora Tora," then purchased by Jim Matthews, president of International Flight Research in Winter Park, Florida. Matthews frequently flies the Zero for his own amusement, and is always ready to contribute a colorful buzz or two during parades and at patriotic gatherings. Jimmie Doolittle, who commanded the famous "Thirty Seconds Over Tokyo" bomber raid, particularly cherished a fly-by salute from Matthews and his Zero several years ago when the little general was honored at Florida Institute of Technology in Melbourne.

An original Piper Cub, a 1930 Butler Blackhawk, a 1944 Beech Stagger Wing, a 1940 Steerman and a World War II PT-19 Primary Trainer are just a handful of the other aircrafts parked here.

Most of the flying is done on weekends, but any time during daylight hours is a good time to visit and look. But please, do not touch the merchandise. That's all friendly Bob White asks of visitors. He does no advertising. He has no souvenir stands, no concessions, and charges no admission fees. His telephone number is (305) 886-3180.

It's an aviator's dream.

The Way to Go: North on US 441 to Zellwood. Or east on Interstate 4, and take the Altamonte Springs-Apopka exit. Turn left on US 436. This brings you through Forest City, Apopka, Plymouth and into Zellwood. Turn left (west) at Jones Avenue and drive a mile to the dirt road entrance (on the right) to the airstrip. Less than a 45-minute drive from downtown Orlando.

Florida Agriculture

Once upon a time, and not too long ago at that, you could come to this section of Florida, knock on the door of a citrus processing plant, or show up unexpectedly at one of the other agricultural spreads, and receive a warm welcome and a tour of the premises.

Times have changed.

But don't blame the agricultural industry. Those folks have not turned their backs on the public. No, the fault lies in stiffer insurance rates. Companies naturally need protection when the public comes trudging through their compounds at odd intervals, and with stricter restrictions and rocketing insurance rates, it's no longer feasible for them to accommodate visitors.

Except in certain circumstances.

Farm Tours of Florida is one of the exceptions. This company, based in the little community of Zellwood, has packaged a three-hour, movie-and-bus tour that gives visitors a close-up look at the little daily miracles produced by the good earth of

Central Florida.

But please note: These narrated tours of 28,000 acres of Zellwood muck farms and greenhouses are offered only during the months of December, January, February and March.

Approximately an hour of the tour is devoted to movies, featuring the film, *Seeds to Salad*, which traces the development of the kind of seeds planted here, from bloom to supermarket display. Another hour is spent on vegetables farms, and a third hour in 23 greenhouses over about 20 acres, a veritable bonanza for picture takers.

It can get very cold in Central Florida during winter months; but the bus, theater and greenhouses are climate-controlled.

Zellwood mucklands on the shore of Lake Apopka are rejuvenated by flooding between crops. Separating the lake and farming area are 10 miles of muck levee. The levee, for the record, is 74 feet above sea level, the lake 66 feet and soil 62 feet.

This is where you see miles of winter vegetables, such as cabbage, cauliflower, radishes, lettuce and many others—including 11,000 acres of carrots, a strong winter staple in the produce department.

Corn? Of course. An estimated 10,000 acres of the famous Zellwood sweet corn are planted in March and April, and 2.5 million crates are harvested in May and June. The annual Zellwood Sweet Corn Festival, usually held the first weekend in June, attracts more than 100,000 people.

One of the authentic superstars of the area is Zellwin Farms, started in 1947 on 600 acres in Zellwood on Lake Apopka. Today it covers 4,400 acres, one of the biggest truck farms in the South, and one of the few remaining family owned and operated commercial agricultural enterprises. Each year, by double cropping, Zellwin produces the equivalent of 7,000 acres of vegetables (radishes, cantaloupes, corn, cauliflower, leek, anise, cabbage, lettuce, carrots, etc.) and, in peak season, hires about 800 employees.

Zellwin is a self-sufficient farm. Much of the custom-built equipment in daily use has been conceived, designed and developed right here. Grumann Ag aircraft seem to be in the air constantly tending the fields. A customized loading system, pioneered by Zellwin, allows trucks to be loaded in any combination of 27 crops. The one-stop loading reduces transportation costs, raises profit margins for brokers and keeps retail costs at a minimum. American farms are far ahead of the world in farming technology, and Zellwin Farms is an ideal example of why that's so.

There's not as much crop production to observe at Zellwin in July and August, although the flooding of the mucklands between crops to maintain soil productivity, control weeds and soil borne disease, and to prevent excessive oxidation, is as interesting to some folks as anything else that takes place in this remarkable location. Muck, for the benefit of city folks, is a layer of peat-based soil about five feet thick and a few feet below normal lake level. During the floodings, an unbelievable variety of birds are attracted here, and bird watchers from miles around come flocking in.

Also, for the record, the city of Apopka, a short drive to the south of Zellwood, is known as the foliage capital of the world. The industry claims to contribute more to the economy of Orange County than citrus. Both industries, however, were hurt critically by recent freezes.

From December 1 to April 1, Farm Tours busses leave Zellwood at 9 a.m. and 1:30 p.m., Mondays through Fridays, regardless of the number of passengers. The cost is $7 per person, half that for children. Management says your money will be refunded if you're not satisfied with the 20-mile tour.

Questions, anyone? Write to Farm Tours, Box 718, Zellwood, FL 32798. Or call (305) 886-8544 or (305) 886-4729.

The Way to Go: North on US 441 to Zellwood. Or east on Interstate 4, and take the Altamonte Springs-Apopka exit. Turn left on US 436. The highway cuts into 441 in Apopka, then straight into Zellwood. From downtown Orlando, about a half-hour's drive.

Holy Trinity Church in Fruitland Park. Photo by Ray Powell.

Holy Trinity Episcopal Church

About two miles north of Fruitland Park in Lake County, fringed by tall pines and oak trees dripping with Spanish moss, stands a quaint little Gothic church built in 1888 with funds sent from England.

This is Holy Trinity Episcopal Church, a parish in the diocese of Central Florida, and recently added to the National Register of Historic Places. You've got to see it. There's a majestic simplicity about the church that transcends the leanings of any particular religious denomination.

Established by a colony of English citrus grove owners and workers, this was once a lonely setting. Somehow, though, despite the encroachment of new homes, the Holy Trinity grounds manage to maintain a withdrawn atmosphere, presenting a page of history as well as a tranquil place to worship. It's a 10-acre spread, much of it yielding to a graveyard.

The first unusual photographic possibility a visitor notices is the ancient, covered lych-gate—one of the two existing today in the United States—at the side entrance. In days gone by it was used only for funerals. This is where the clergyman waited as the procession paused for a few moments of reflection, then led the family into church for funeral services. Today this station of heavy memories summons the past and the present into peaceful sanctuary.

Because of the exquisite trappings and vaulted ceiling, the interior of the fresh-white church reminds one of a miniature cathedral. It's constructed of Florida pine so hard that you can try in vain to drive a nail into it. Below the three-paneled stained-glass window is a mahogany, handmade altar. About 10 o'clock in the morning is the best time to see the windows filter the fullness of the sun's rays. At such times the Good Shepherd seems to step from the center glass and into the church. One parishioner was so moved by the beauty of the scene that he had a statue fashioned from it, and it now stands in the churchyard cemetery.

One of the most prominent tombstones here is marked with the name William Reed Newell (1868–1956), composer of the revered hymn, "At Calvary." He was the father of two prominent men now living in nearby Leesburg, the Rev. Philip R. Newell, director of the Great Commission Prayer League and former dean of students at Moody Bible Institute in Chicago; and novelist David M. Newell.

For years the doors of Holy Trinity Episcopal Church were never locked. Parishioners and others could come in at any hour of day or night whenever they needed a quiet place of meditation, supplication or thanksgiving, but now, dismayingly, because of recent acts of vandalism, the church is mostly locked. Best time to visit any time of year is Sunday morning, say from about 7 o'clock until noon, and there's a 10 a.m. service on Wednesday. Occasionally there's a wedding or some other activity on the grounds on Saturday. The office next door is open Monday through Thursday from 1:15 p.m. to 5 p.m.

Mailing address: Holy Trinity Episcopal Church, PO Box 435, Fruitland Park, FL 32731. Telephone (with 24-hour answering service): (904) 787-1500.

The Way to Go: Take the Apopka-Altamonte Springs exit off Interstate 4, turn left. This is Route 436 (Semoran Boulevard), and it joins Route 441 in Apopka. Continue north on 441 to Fruitland Park. Watch for the Florida Highway Patrol station on the left about two miles farther along on 441, and make a left at the next turn, Spring Lake Road. There's a convenience store on the corner. The church is not quite a mile up the road on the right. From downtown Orlando: about 51 miles.

Marion County Horse Farms

Marion County. Horse breeding country. Home of famous thoroughbreds. Thousands of grassy soft acres spreading and rolling under the warm sun as far as the eye can see.

Welcome to the green slice of Florida.

Welcome to God's big acres.

Owners and trainers at the more than two dozen prominent horse farms in Marion County don't mind bragging that their kingdom now ranks with Kentucky and California as a prime center in the production of prized thoroughbreds; and they can offer the names of such race track superstars as Needles, Carry Back, Affirmed, Foolish Pleasure, Dr. Fager, Susan's Pleasure and Codex as proof.

Most of the farms open their gates to visitors, although there are no guided tours unless some special provisions are made far in advance. Even so, there's plenty to ogle as you drive leisurely through the main roads of the farms. Ownerships and regulations do change; therefore it's suggested you drive into Ocala and visit the Ocala/Marion County Chamber of Commerce to obtain all the up-to-date information on locations and visitation rights.

The chamber is at 110 E. Silver Springs Road (a well-marked and heavily-traveled thoroughfare), downtown facing the square, five blocks east of US 441. Telephone: (904) 629-8051. Another place where visitors find a warm welcome is the Hall of Fame in the Florida Thoroughbred Breeders Association office at the Golden Hills Golf & Turf Club, seven miles west of Ocala on US 27. Oil paintings of the more renowned Florida-bred thoroughbreds hang here.

Let's take a look at Tartan Farms as an example of a spread that allows visitors. They proudly call it the thoroughbred breeding farm of champions (Codex, Dr. Fager, In Reality, etc.). Take the SR 200 exit from Interstate 75, drive west approximately two miles to SW 66th Street (old Williams Road), then hang

Thoroughbreds and luscious green acres abound in the Florida horse country of Marion County.

another left for another mile and a half or so. Driving tours are encouraged on Monday through Friday only, from 9 a.m. to noon, and again from 1 p.m. to 3 p.m. Visitors are not permitted to get out of their cars. The tour usually takes about 30 minutes. No admission charge.

Some point to the friendly climate as the cardinal reason that the territory of Marion County has developed so phenomenally as a horse farm industry. Others say it's that certain something in the soil, coupled with pure air and pure water. But let's not overlook the pioneering, vision and hard work of the breeders themselves.

It's worth checking out.

* * *

Special note to specialized horse lovers. Komoko Miniature Horse Farm is located in Newberry, 10 miles west of Gainesville, and Gainesville is about 37 miles north of Ocala. The American Miniature is a horse—not a pony—even though its average size is only between 26 inches and 30 inches. Unfortunately, Komoko is not equipped to employ an open-gate policy for visitors. However, if you're really aching to see these horses, or if you're considering buying one for a pet, call the owner, Joel Bridges, (904) 472-2828, to make an appointment. The Kentucky-bred Bridges, once in the funeral business in south Florida, turned his little horse hobby into the biggest breeding farm of its kind in the country. At this writing he has more than 500 of the animals on his 400 acres. He ships 'em all over the world.

The Way to Go: North on US 441, or north on the Florida Turnpike (toll road) and Interstate 75. Ocala is approximately 75 miles from Orlando. The drive on 441 is slower but more interesting.

Marjorie Kinnan Rawlings State Historic Site

"Cross Creek is a bend in a country road, by land, and the flowing of Lochloosa Lake into Orange Lake, by water. We are four miles west of the small village of Island Grove, nine miles east of a turpentine still, and on the other sides we do not count distance at all, for the two lakes, and the broad marshes, create an infinite space between us and the horizons."

Upon entering the Marjorie Kinnan Rawlings home you can read the above classic lines, exactly as the author typed them herself on a sheet of first draft yellow paper on her old Underwood upright. The typewriter—as both vigil and monument—stands on a table on the screened porch of her home which the State of Florida has proudly designated an official historic site.

Marjorie Kinnan Rawlings had tried her hand at serious writing before moving to Cross Creek in 1928, but it was here, smitten by the land, its people and animals, that she found her literary voice. She spoke for the Florida backwoods and surfaced as one of America's foremost authors. Her novel *The Yearling,* focusing on a boy coming of age in these quiet, hidden tracts of marsh and scrub, was awarded a Pulitzer Prize. *Cross Creek, Cross Creek Cookery, South Moon Under, When the Whippoorwill,* and *The Secret River* are among her other fondly remembered book titles.

"When I came here I put all thought of popular writing behind me," Mrs. Rawlings stated. "I was determined to try to interpret the people who so charmed me. If I failed, I would write no more." She attained literary excellence *and* popularity, topped by the Pulitzer in 1939.

Here, visitors also have occasion to inspect a typical late 19th century "Florida cracker" house. Because of the intense, humid summer heat in this part of the world, porches, breezeways and numerous windows were essential. But there were times, too, when the onerous damp weather could—and still can—chill a person's marrow. On such days of winter the kitchen, with its blend of warmth and arresting aroma, would have been the most inviting room of the Rawlings house. Fireplaces heated the bedrooms.

Over the years Mrs. Rawlings contributed structural improvements to her simply furnished home, adding such luxuries as bathrooms. The foundation of the homemade table on the front porch (her favorite writing place) is a cabbage palm log. Even after she married Norton Baskin (her second husband) in 1941, and established a home in St. Augustine, Cross Creek remained a retreat where she could sit at her typewriter and creatively record her feelings of the land, sharing with the world the unaffected triumphs, sorrow and humor—and recipes—of her neighbors. Capturing this regional flavor so convincingly was all the more remarkable when considering her background: Phi Beta Kappa at the University of Wisconsin, and a successful newspaper career in Rochester, New York.

Marjorie Kinnan Rawlings died in 1953 at the age of 57. She was buried near her home at her beloved Cross Creek.

The home is open daily from 9 a.m. to 5 p.m. Visitors over the age of 5 are asked to pay a 50-cent admission fee. Additional information is obtainable by writing: Marjorie Kinnan Rawlings State Historic Site, Route 3, Box 92, Hawthorne, Florida 32640. Or by phoning: (904) 466-3672.

* * *

Meal tip: Alligator meat—yes, authentic Florida alligator meat—is part of the regular menu at the Yearling Restaurant, a minute's drive beyond the Rawlings Home. The meat is cut into bite sizes and deep fried. Don't be surprised if some of the bites are a bit chewy. The Yearling is closed on Monday.

The Way to Go: North on US 441, then continue ahead on US 301 out of Ocala to Island Grove, watch for sign and turn left, and drive four miles. Or north on the Florida Turnpike (toll road) and Interstate 75, then cut across east to Ocala and US

301. The Marjorie Kinnan Rawlings State Historic Site is about 20 miles south of Gainesville. Roundtrip from Orlando: approximately 200 miles.

Mount Dora

You see it on bumper stickers and T-shirts: "I Climbed Mt. Dora."

It's a little joke in these parts, perhaps a tired little joke by now, but the one-liner seldom fails to draw a quick smile from those who haven't seen it or heard it before.

Mount Dora, of course, is not a mountain or even a foothill. Mount Dora is a town of fewer than 7,000 residents in Lake County, but it was built on a bluff overlooking Lake Dora at an elevation of 184 feet above sea level—one of the highest community elevations in Florida.

Because of the hilly terrain, mammoth oak trees and buildings of northern design, Mount Dora is called "The New England of the South." There is no village square, but the downtown village, with distinctive lampposts, flower-filled brick planters, and its many and varied shops, creates an atmosphere found nowhere else on the peninsula. Mount Dora is also called "Everyone's Hometown," "The Rose Capital of Cental Florida," "The Antique Center of Central Florida," and "Serenity Without Isolation." A recent national survey also pinpointed the community as one of the safest in which to live.

Mount Dora is 25 miles northwest of Orlando, cuddled among hills, expansive citrus groves, tropical foliage and lakes. It's doubtful you'll want to verify this, but Lake County has 1,400 lakes—and each one is named.

As you turn off US 441 and follow Old US 441 North, you get the feeling of a different geographic flavor at once. The highway bends and climbs toward the city limits. Off to the right is the eye-catching, immaculate white, old, New England-styled church where a predominately black congregation worships. A bit farther along on the right, on an elevated plateau, is St. Patrick's Roman Catholic Church, comparatively small and

A sailboat drifts across Lake Dora, with the town of Mount Dora—
"The New England of the South"—visible in the background.

modern, with a scattering of tiny, squared, stained-glass windows behind the altar, quite the inspirational sight when they catch the afternoon sun. St. Patrick's is open during the day to visitors.

Once inside the city limits, watch for 5th Avenue, and turn left. This is a continuation of Old US 441, taking visitors on the final mile downtown. The first eye-catcher here is an historic, three-story, sparkling white Victorian home that looks like a giant wedding cake, and is currently utilized by a masonic lodge. It's located just north of the hub intersection, 5th Avenue and Donnelly Street, across from the landmark Shuffleboard Club.

This is the heart of the downtown. Take in the restaurants, hardware and book stores; drugstore; shops and boutiques bulging with gifts, antiques, crafts and fashions; real estate offices and the office of the *Mount Dora Topic,* a respected weekly newspaper. Off 5th Avenue and down a sort of alley alongside Romer's Bakery is the Royellou Museum, maintained by the Mount Dora Historical Society. It's probably the smallest museum you'll come across in Florida, and it's open only on Wednesday (2–4 p.m.) and Saturday (10 a.m.–4 p.m.), but it's a vault of area history and intriguing exhibits. The building itself, the old city jail, stands as a museum. A few of the exhibits are set up in the old cells, and you can see a hole where some prisoners once crawled to freedom.

For its size, Mount Dora has an outstanding public library—on the corner of Donnelly and 9th Avenue. The city has high-graded schools; exceptionally fine and busy shuffleboard, croquet and lawn bowling facilities; an 18-hole golf course; a 40-doctor hospital; a yacht club; an acclaimed little theater group at the IceHouse Theater; and just about every kind of recreation for young and old. In all, Mount Dora has 13 antique shops. And aside from downtown there are two modern shopping centers with about 40 additional stores. About two dozen different religious denominations are also represented.

Launch your boat from a ramp at Gilbert Park, and, by circuitous connecting waterways, it's possible to sail almost anywhere in the world.

One of Mount Dora's most conspicuous edifices is a century-old winter resort, the Lakeside Inn, where President and Mrs. Calvin Coolidge vacationed for a month in 1930. Located across from the Chamber of Commerce's office in the restored railroad depot downtown, the hotel has undergone significant building additions and renovations, and now offers 110 bedrooms with top-drawer service. Lakeside Inn is owned and managed by Dick Edgerton, son of an early pioneer in the area. Edgerton, like so many of the oldtimers and more recent permanent residents, is an active participant in the town's civic arena.

Mount Dora was nearly turned upside down and inside out in the summer of 1980 when a feature motion picture company moved in to film scenes for the high-budgeted movie "Honky Tonk Freeway." An inundation of tourists and gawkers followed, and not all the local residents were tickled about the two months of drastic disorder in their town routine, or in seeing downtown store fronts being painted pink for the filming. It was estimated, though, that close to $1 million was spent here during the short "Hollywood season," and that's quite a hype in any community's economic arm.

Mount Dora hosts an overrun of visitors in February also during the annual Art Festival, but this is easier to take because it lasts only a weekend. Not that Mount Dora doesn't cater to visitors. It's a friendly town. They don't seek isolation—just their priceless serenity.

The Way to Go: North on US 441 all the way. Or go by way of Interstate 4 North. Get off on the Altamonte Springs-Apopka exit, then turn left. This is Route 436, and it hooks up with 441 in Apopka. Drive through Apopka, Plymouth and Zellwood, and turn left on Old 441 North, the entranceway into Mount Dora. It's about 30 miles from downtown Orlando to downtown Mount Dora, approximately 45 minutes to drive.

Ocala
National Forest

Wilderness by the thousands of acres. Longleaf pine, cypress, dwarf liveoak, pine hardwood swamp, and the biggest area of sand pine in the world. Lakes, streams, springs, White-tailed deer, squirrel, quail, raccoon, bear, cottontail. Yes, alligators and snakes too. Maybe a few endangered Florida panthers along the way. Birds, birds, birds. Campgrounds, recreation areas, swimming, fishing, boating. You can even go in and cut your own Christmas tree.

A capsulized paragraph does it scant justice, and yet, fundamentally, that's what the Ocala National Forest is.

The Ocala. The Big Scrub. The oldest national forest east of the Mississippi River, and the southernmost national forest in the country. Hike it, paddle it, drive it. Measure your own enjoyment.

Perhaps the best way to see this protected land and to experience its mysteries is to hike the Ocala Trail—but a few words of caution, if you please. If you're inexperienced at this kind of recreation, don't try to tackle too much in one outing. After all, this trail is 66 miles long. Wear comfortable clothing and comfortably tough shoes; take a trial trek of an hour or so. Then one day, after conditioning yourself, when you can spare a week and want to withdraw from the swiftness and pressures of civilization, go all the way. The winding trail of grass, pine needles and boardwalks guides you past 60 natural ponds, brings you close to eight recreation areas, draws you deeper and deeper into the heart of the great outdoors from sunup to sundown and through the night.

Whether it's a short or long hike: Stay on the trail! It's well marked. Orange paint blazed on trees shows the way. If you walk more than 100 yards without sighting a blaze, turn back. You wouldn't be the first person ever to get lost in the forest. Blue blazes mark the side trails, showing the way to water and campsites.

Summer in Ocala is not the best time to go hiking. The weather can be—and almost always is—oppressively hot and humid. The area gets most of its rain in summer. Late afternoon cloudbursts are almost daily happenings, and the moisture feeds the mosquitoes and other insects (including a tiny bug the Indians called no-see-ums). Insect repellent and a snake bite kit should be part of your equipment.

Well, there are any number of vital items to fill a backpack, so the neophyte hiker, or those approaching foreign soil for the first time, should pull in at the Seminole Ranger District office, just north of Eustis on Route 19, for maps, hunting season times and sundry tips. However, the office is closed weekends. You can write to Seminole Ranger District, PO Box 1360, Eustis, FL 32726; or call (904) 357-3721. This is also the office where you can obtain a free permit to select and chop down your own Christmas tree.

Another Forest Service source is Lake George Ranger District, Post Office Building, PO Box 1206, Ocala, FL 32670. Then there are the Lake Bryant Ranger Station, 18 miles east of Ocala on Route 40; and Pittman Ranger Station, 11 miles north of Eustis on Route 19.

For information on those portions of the Florida Trail not in the forest, write the Florida Trail Association, 4410 N.W. 18th Place, Gainesville, FL 32605. Plans are mapped for the Florida Trail eventually to stretch across the 700-mile span of Florida.

There are roads and good highways in the Ocala National Forest, so visitors don't necessarily have to "rough it" to draw their year-round enjoyment. Alexander Springs Recreation Area at the lower eastern end of the forest is recommended for first-time visitors, or those with only a day or a few hours to spend. There's a small admission charge.

It's located 16 miles north of Eustis on Route 19, a natural semitropical complex of rustic beauty, centered around Alexander Springs which discharges nearly 80 million gallons of water daily at a constant temperature of 72 degrees. Facilities: picnic tables and shelters, fireplaces, trailer spaces (no sewer or electrical hookups but there is a central dumping station for trailer holding tanks), tent camping area, telephones, restrooms, swimming, bathhouse, concession stand, rental canoes, and a self-guided interpretive walk through exotic junglelike paths. A spur trail connects with the Ocala Trail. Game fishing in the clear waters of Spring Creek is usually quite productive. Licenses required.

Write Alexander Springs Recreation Area, PO Box 11, Altoona, FL 32702.

The Ocala, established November 24, 1908, and Florida's sister forests to the north, the Apalachicola and the Osceola, are part of the 174 National Forests and National Grasslands totalling 187 million acres in 44 states and Puerto Rico, equal to an area about the size of Great Britain and France combined. The U.S. Congress decreed that these National Forests and their renewable resources—water, timber, wildlife, forage for cattle, and recreation—should be managed and protected under the doctrine of wise, multiple use and sustained yield, by Americans and for Americans of today and the future.

The Way to Go: North on US 441 (North Orange Blossom Trail) to Eustis. Turn north on Route 19. Driving time: about an hour.

St. Augustine

You can travel from Orlando, spend a full day here in the nation's oldest city, and still be back before nightfall. But you'll be tempted to stay over—it's that irresistible.

There are admission charges at some of the commercial attractions, such as Ripley's Believe It Or Not Museum, the Old Jail, Potter's Wax Museum and the Oldest Store Museum; but it's possible to see and do enough in this city without upsetting the family budget—depending, of course, on how much you eat and drink, and on how many souvenirs you'll want to cart home.

To get your bearings, check in first at the visitors information center, (904) 829-5681, at 10 Castillo Drive near the city gates. While there, view the 15-minute sound-color movie about the area. The information mailing address is St. Augustine and St. Johns County Chamber of Commerce, PO Box 0, St. Augustine, FL 32085.

Colorful back streets hold unhurried memories and charm of old St. Augustine.

Here's a fast fact to excite even the lukewarm history buff: St. Augustine was founded 55 years before the Pilgrims hit shore at Plymouth Rock. You can stroll down the narrow and picturesque streets of the restoration area, and get a feel of those times of 300 years ago, and study the lifestyles and crafts in the myriad historic homes and buildings.

Although St. Augustine was founded by the Spanish in 1565, there is a colorful blend of English and American heritage here, fortified by traditional Southern hospitality. No matter your religious affiliation, or lack of it, don't miss the Cathedral of St. Augustine, or the Mission of Nombre de Dios (Shrine of Our Lady of La Leche, where the first Catholic Mass was celebrated in the United States), or the Trinity Episcopal Church.

And don't leave St. Augustine without first inspecting the great fort that frowns awesomely on the sea as if it's remembering those two unsuccessful sieges by the English. Construction of the fort, Castillo de San Marcos, was begun in 1672, a century before the American Revolution. Built basically of coquina (a shell rock formation found in the area), the fort was never captured by an enemy. Admission is only 50 cents (at this writing) for adults; children under 16 admitted free if accompanied by an adult.

Any season is excellent for visiting St. Augustine, but remember that *Cross and Sword,* the official state play that dramatically re-creates the founding of the city, is performed only from June 16 through August 30 (Tuesday–Saturday, 8:30 p.m.; call (904) 824-1965 for information and reservations).

Neglected by most visitors as refreshing stopoffs are Favor-Dykes State Park, 15 miles south of St. Augustine, east of U.S. 1; and Washington Oakes, about 10 miles south of the city of A1A. Both have beautiful gardens and picnic areas.

The Way to Go: East on Interstate 4 out of Orlando; then north on Interstate 95 toward Jacksonville. Round trip from Orlando: about 200 miles.

Stephen Foster Center

White Springs is a long haul from Orlando, but you can make it up and back in a day and still spend enough time here to savor all the flavor and nostalgia of "Old Folks At Home."

The Stephen Foster Center in. White Springs is a non-commercial attraction developed by the state as testimonial to one of America's finest composers; spread out in a park of 250 wooded, gingerly-landscaped acres. Stephen Foster's "Old Folks At Home," equally well known as "Suwanee River," has been officially adopted as the state song, but it's more than words and music: it manifests here as a colorful page of Florida history.

White Springs is North Florida country, and the center itself is sufficient cause for Central Floridians and outsiders to come see what living is like in this part of the state. It's just three miles off Interstate 75, and makes a refreshing pick-up for travelers going in or out of Georgia. Plan to spend at least an hour and a half.

Foster Museum is the focal point of the center. Designed as an ante-bellum mansion, it's furnished with delightful and priceless exhibits, including eight dioramas-animated presentations of favorite Foster songs, original manuscripts, historical dolls and old musical instruments. There are two more dioramas in the base of the striking, 200-foot Carillon Tower, plus Foster era trappings, and a rare, German-made piano which the composer is said to have often played at a neighbor's home. Daily carillon concerts are offered from the tower.

There are picnic tables throughout the park, many of them under ancient live oak trees overlooking the famous river. There's a pavilion for picnickers and a refreshment counter. Admission to the center is 50 cents. The center is open every day from 9 a.m. to 5 p.m. Address inquiries to Stephen Foster Center, White Springs, FL 32096. Telephone: (904) 397-1556.

While here you should take the time to board one of the two 30-passenger replicas of early river boats for a ride up the

Suwanee. There's an extra charge of $1 for the river ride. There are no exotic plants or wild animals to see along the way: it's simply a pleasant 20-minute excursion—and then you can always tell the old folks at home that you've been on the Suwanee River.

Stephen Foster was born in Lawrenceville, Pennsylvania, (near Pittsburgh) on July 4, 1826. Although he visited the South only once, some of his best known musical works were sentimental Southern ballads like "My Old Kentucky Home," "Old Black Joe," "Jeanie With The Light Brown Hair" and "Beautiful Dreamer." His first published song was "Open Thy Lattice, Love," but his first hit composition was "Oh! Susanna" in 1848. For all his success and enduring fame, Stephen Foster died penniless in New York City at the age of 37.

The Way to Go: Take the Florida Turnpike north. It branches off to Interstate 75 near Wildwood. Continue north on the interstate, and exit at Route 136, and drive east for three miles to White Springs. You're now just about 50 miles from the Georgia border. Orlando to White Springs: 170 miles.

Wekiwa Springs State Park

Don't be befuddled by the spelling. Wekiwa sometimes turns up as Wekiva on signs in these parts.

Spelled either way, the Indian word means "spring of water," most authorities agree.

And spelled either way, this state-guarded area, just 17 miles from downtown Orlando, offers 6,400 acres of wild scenery, and a sanctuary for picnickers, swimmers, canoeists, hikers and nature buffs in general. Most area residents come here in summer, but in so doing they miss the best time of all in the woods: late fall, winter and early spring, before the buildup of the insect population and muggy weather.

Whatever your pleasure, whatever the season, Wekiwa Springs State Park is one of the finest, close-in opportunities to experience the Central Florida as it was in the days when the Timucuan Indians had the run of the land.

The park is situated along the eastern slope of the high sandy ridge which extends down the center of Florida, and embraces varied elevations, vegetation, soil types, geologic formations and animals. Beautiful Wekiwa Springs is formed by water flowing from beneath the central ridge through limestone caverns. The spring is the chief source of the Wekiwa River, which links with Rock Springs Run and empties into the St. Johns River 15 miles away to the northeast.

Streams form the north and east boundary of the park. The wet forest bordering the streams is called river swamp, an area supporting such hardwoods as tupelo, maple, ash, sweetgum and bald cypress, and such wildlife as otters, raccoons, alligators, turtles, limpkins, herons and egrets.

Advancing to the higher elevations, you come across laurel and water oaks, needle and sabal palms. Called the "hydrick hammock," the region is subject to a share of the dampness, though seldom flooded. Owls and woodpeckers spend a lot of time here. On even higher ground bordering the hammocks you begin to see the pond and slash pine trees, and an overrun of palmetto and fetterbrush. A self-guiding trail leads from the wetlands through the longleaf pine forests to the stands of sand pine scrub at Sand Lake picnic grounds.

The sand pine scrub here is unique to Florida; and naturally breeds and feeds (with help from the ubiquitous oak trees) species of animals living nowhere else. Examples: Florida mouse, Florida worm lizard, gopher frog, sand skink, and the scrub jay.

Too infrequently do Central Florida residents bother to study the living landscape at their backdoor, and this land virtually throbs with the drama of nature. The pine flatwoods furnish an excellent illustration. Rainfall is a daily happening in summer, but as winter approaches and the dryness spreads its brittle blanket, fire replaces flooding as a shaping force of the earth. Fire, the result of lightning, is accepted as a natural force.

Vegetation here—in one of those acts of nature we label minor miracles—has adapted by developing a mysterious method of preventing permanent fire damage. Indeed, the survival of some species depends on frequent burning.

The geologic order of the forest also reveals something about the imperceptible, somewhat spooky depths beneath our feet. Most of the state sits on an uneasy foundation of limestone which has cracked at various times and places. Water flowing through these cracks dissolves the limestone and creates deep chambers in the earth. When the ceiling of the chamber becomes so threadbare that it can support the sand above it no longer, the ceiling caves in and a sinkhole is formed.

Occasionally in Florida we read in the newspaper about someone's backyard getting sucked into the earth, or about a house sinking gradually into the ground. Several years ago in Orlando an elementary school cafeteria sank into a crater—not out of sight, but so deeply that the walls collapsed and the building had to be replaced entirely. It wasn't such a slow process either. One morning when the milk delivery man made his rounds, the cafeteria just wasn't there. The obvious funnel-shaped depressions in the uplands of Wekiwa are sinkholes, a number of which have filled with water to form lakes and ponds. Lake Prevatt, biggest lake in the park, is an example.

Every so often park rangers report the sighting of a black bear or a Southern bald eagle. The grey fox, raccoon, squirrel, swamp rabbit, possum and bobcat are more common. Deer range from the sandhills, down through the flatwoods to the hammocks and swamps. There's a chance you'll see a deer on the scenic drive. Migrating waterfowl flock here in winter.

Wekiwa Springs State Park opens every day at 8 a.m., and closes at sundown. There's a charge of 50 cents for admission. Those under the age of 6 admitted free. Call (305) 889-3140 for details and all information. Or write Wekiwa Springs State Park, 1800 Wekiwa Circle, Apopka, FL 32703.

The Way to Go: Take the Apopka-Altamonte Springs exit off Interstate 4. Turn left on Route 436 (Semoran Boulevard). Watch for the state park sign on the right after driving through Forest City. Turn right and drive another three miles to the park entrance. It's on the left. Driving time: 20 minutes.

Walt Disney World Village

It's part of Disney World; but Walt Disney World Village is really another world.

First, a word about the unique vacation complex at Lake Buena Vista. Located several miles from the unseen, celebrated Magic Kingdom, on the eastern apron of the huge Disney property, in a setting of grasslands, gardens, lakes and vistas, the complex offers resort hotels, vacation villas, a conference center, an office park, outdoor recreation, and the hub of the community: the Shopping Village.

Free-wheeling pedestrian streets and flower-bordered paths wind around craft stores, eating facilities, and more than two dozen shops featuring books, candy, ceramics, china, and glassware, designer fashions, vintage wines, plants, rare antiques and priceless imports, souvenirs, arts, jewelry, toys, a pottery chalet and a variety of other wares. There's a gourmet pantry, delicatessen, bakery, and an old-fashioned Ice Cream Fountain.

Shady walkways curve around Buena Vista Lagoon where the stately and graceful Empress Lilly Riverboat Restaurant is permanently anchored. Aboard the sprightly, shiny old boat, diners may choose the Fishermen's Deck, Steerman's Quarters, or the French cuisine in the elegant Empress Room. Then there's non-stop musical entertainment nightly in the Baton Rouge Lounge. Picture taking is a popular activity on top deck.

Other pleasant dining places: Village Verandah, Cap'n Jack's Oyster Bar and Village Restaurant. Close-by, the Lake Buena

Vista Club has another good dining room, plus a lounge and an 18-hole championship golf course with tennis, swimming and other recreation.

Music for jazz enthusiasts is a regular feature at the Village Lounge. Contemporary music is the style at the four high-rise resort hotels—Howard Johnson's Motor Inn, TraveLodge Tower, Dutch Inn and Royal Plaza—located at Lake Buena Vista Hotel Plaza along the slightly divided parkway entrance to the Shopping Village. The inventive, master-planned community of Lake Buena Vista also encompasses 133 vacation villas for overnight rental, 60 two-bedroom treehouses snuggled into woodlands beside golf course fairways, 64 villas along the course, and 136 villas at the conference center.

It's the Shopping Village, though, that rates the attention and the recommendation here, a pick-you-up kind of place in which to shop or browse unhurriedly, or to watch the little rented putt-putt boats on the lagoon, or to observe the parade of strollers from Central Florida, from around the country and across the seas. The colorful promenade is endless.

The spacious Village, paved to accommodate wheelchairs, is open every day from 10 a.m. to 10 p.m., and there are acres of free parking. No admission charge. Spend only if you wish to do so. Mailing address: Walt Disney World Village, Lake Buena Vista, FL 32830. The Disney telephone number: (305) 824-2222.

You might encounter a group of wandering musicians at the Village, or catch an art show or a special outdoor demonstration or program, or bump into a visiting movie star or one of the famous entertainers who appear regularly in Orlando and at Disney's Top Of The World in the Contemporary Resort Hotel. There always seems to be a little extra something going on at the Village, and all of it marked with the unmistakably fastidious touch of Disney.

The Way to Go: Take the Kissimmee-Lake Buena Vista-SR 535 exit off Interstate 4. The exit is 15 miles from downtown Orlando. Head north on 535, but jockey quickly to the left-turn lane. Turn left at the first traffic light (the entrance is well marked), and cruise another mile to the Village parking area. Driving time: about 20 minutes.

Mountain Lake
Sanctuary

Visitors call it an experience, not a place. Some say it's one of the most serene locations on the face of the globe. It's Mountain Lake Sanctuary at Lake Wales, dramatically set in almost the exact geographic center of the state.

Most Florida residents refer to the area as the Bok Singing Tower because of the 255-foot stone structure that stands as the area's focal and artistic point. The "voice" of the Tower is a 53-bronze bell carillon that emits a rare sound of music every half-hour; and then there's a 45-minute recital played every day at 3 p.m. When the carillon is playing, the entire structure seems alive with musical vibrations. Benches are scattered throughout the park for your restful listening pleasure.

The 130-acre park, with its reflection pool, groves, fine vistas and pathways, is lovingly pampered by the landscaping crew. The grounds, whispering with serenity, are picture perfect. Nowhere is there evidence that this was once a sandy hill cluttered with pines and scrub palmettos.

As you stroll through the sanctuary and Pine Ridge Nature Reserve (a brisk walk seems almost indecent in these surroundings), you can see an enchanting collection of ferns and palms, a lily garden, wild grass and wild flowers, camphor trees, berries, myriad varieties of azaleas (they bloom from November to April), colorful birds, exotic fish and small animals. In short, the sanctuary is a living museum of much that is cultivated, wild and wonderful.

The squirrels along the pathways are plump and brassy little beggars. They come up and practically ask for handouts. If you don't pay attention to them they're liable to tug at your slack or try climbing your leg.

The sanctuary, once a sacred ground where Seminoles came to worship, is located at the top of Iron Mountain and is part of the ridge of Central Florida. The altitude is 259 feet. (Disregard the height of 324 feet as inscribed on the bronze entrance plaque. That figure was taken from an early, incorrect survey. Regardless, people here still claim it's Florida's highest elevation.)

Edward Bok, a Dutch immigrant and world-famous publisher, bought this property just outside the northeastern rim of the city of Lake Wales, and in 1923 commissioned Frederick Law Olmsted to transform it into a wildlife sanctuary "that will touch the soul with its beauty and quiet," and then Bok presented it to the American people as a gift. He later added the carillon tower, fashioned after those he recalled from boyhood days in The Netherlands. President Calvin Coolidge dedicated the Singing Tower and Sanctuary in 1929. Interestingly, the railroad cars that transported the giant carillon bells from Philadelphia were assigned closer security than that given Coolidge's Presidential train.

The pink and gray tower is constructed of coquina stone (native to Florida) and marble from Georgia. The music, either taped or live, is performed by the resident carillonneur, Milford Myhre. There's a sundial on the south wall of the tower which should fascinate the more math-minded members of your party. The tower is not open to the public, but if you're interested in knowing what the inside of it looks like, check the drawing in the visitor's center to the left of the restrooms and bulletin board. Wheelchairs and strollers are also available at the center.

The center itself is interesting: it's a converted Florida "cracker" house.

Admission gates to the grounds are open every day from 8 a.m. to 5:30 p.m. Gates are locked at 6:30 p.m. Although there is no admission charge, there's a parking fee of $2 per car. For answers to specific questions, write Mountain Lake Sanctuary, PO Box 268, Lake Wales, FL 33853.

The Way to Go: West on Interstate 4 (toward Tampa). It's about 27 miles from downtown Orlando to the first cutoff at US 27, a right turn on Exit 23. Proceed south on US 27 past Haines City (8 miles) to Route 17A (12 miles), and turn left. Continue on 17A and follow signs. Roundtrip driving time: less than three hours.

Reptile World Serpentarium

Producing snake venom is not your run-of-the-mill business, but that's been the main business of Reptile World Serpentarium since 1972. Opening the facility to the public in 1976 was a sort of afterthought.

Anyone engaged in the production of snake venom for a living can scarcely escape attention, and so with innumerable individuals and groups dropping by to ask permission to look at his exotic workshop, owner George VanHorn decided to rework his facility to accommodate visitors—and set a modest admission fee. It's a neat and informative place to go, and a visitor gets the quick impression that the business is in able hands. Well, it sure is the wrong kind of place to work if one tends to be lax or slipshod.

Ninety per cent of the snake venom produced at Reptile World (about a 20-minute drive east of Disney World) is utilized in bio-medical research, mostly in this country although the product is also shipped to European and Asiatic markets. Visitors are shown and briefed on the touchy laboratory process in regular 30-minute programs, but they're allowed to proceed at their own pace through the serpentarium to examine all the well-marked exhibits.

The collection includes 60 species of reptiles, predominantly snakes, from Florida and around the world. To name a few: 15 species of rattlesnake, four species of cobra, three varieties of Mamba, a whopping boa constrictor, Gila monster and lizards. To see a cobra coil into a defensive position is enough to freeze one's backbone. Visitors are instructed not to taunt the snakes. Such antics cause the snakes to get angry, and that shortens their lives.

The serpentarium is open Tuesday through Sunday from 9 a.m. to 5:30 p.m. Closed on Christmas, four days over Thanksgiving holiday, and all of September. Admissions: $3 plus tax for adults; $2 plus tax for the 6-17 age group. Younger children admitted free when accompanied by a parent. The explanatory programs begin at 11 a.m. each day, and every 90 minutes thereafter.

Mailing address: Reptile World Serpentarium, 4727 E. Space Coast Parkway, St. Cloud, FL 32769. Telephone: (305) 892-6905. 2695.

Like everyone else who comes here you'll probably want to know if the owner of the serpentarium has ever been bitten by one of his snakes. The answer is yes—seven times at last count. But if you're going to be bitten by a snake, this is the right place. Plenty of antitoxin on the premises.

The Way to Go: Take exit 65 from the Florida Turnpike, drive east on US 192 for 10 miles. Reptile World Serpentarium is on the left, four miles east of St. Cloud. Or travel south out of Orlando on US 441 (South Orange Blossom Trail) to Kissimmee. Drive east on US 192 (a continuation of 441) for about 15 miles. About a 70-mile roundtrip.

Spook Hill

Drive your car up to the line clearly marked in the street, shift into neutral, take your foot off the brake, and—

Your car starts to roll . . . backwards . . . uphill!

Does it really? Decide for yourself. Anyway, kids get a big kick out of it, and it's one of Lake Wales' most popular stops. Actually, it's all an optical illusion, but you don't have to tell the kids and spoil the effect.

Optical illusion or not, there are all kinds of legends linked with Spook Hill, mostly Indian lore. Some oldtimers in this eastern portion of Polk County like to tell the tale that the amusing possibilities of this "mysterious" locale were unwittingly discovered by an aged black man who had intended to park his jalopy here while fishing in a nearby lake. When he got out of the car it suddenly started backing uphill. Spooked, he hopped back in and sped away.

Whatever Spook Hill is, it's free.

Spook Hill is not presented here with the endorsement that people should drive all the way from Orlando to experience it, but if you're in Lake Wales to visit one of the more substantial attractions (see Mountain Lake Sanctuary), or just to tour around the city, you really should have a go at the hill.

Lake Wales is a community of slightly more than 10,000 permanent residents. It's called the Crown Jewel of the Ridge, Executive Country, and the Heart of the Holiday Highlands. Take your pick. It's located near the center of the state at an elevation of 250 feet above sea level, making it the highest city in the state. Downtown, renovated several years ago, exudes a feeling of warmth, progress and tranquility. Planners of the new look gave particular attention to incorporating ingress facilities for the disabled.

The Greater Lakes Wales Chamber of Commerce is located in the heart of the downtown Marketplace by the cascading fountain, just off Stuart Avenue. Least complicated way to find the chamber office: turn left of US 27 at the signal light, proceed east into Lake Wales on Central Avenue, and watch for city hall on the right side of the street. You're now a block south of the chamber. Mailing address; PO Box 191, Lake Wales, FL 33853. Telephone: (813) 676-3445.

Lake Wales is also the winter home of the famous Black Hills Passion Play, presented annually, usually from mid-February to mid-April (Easter Sunday), on Tuesday, Thursday, Saturday and Sunday evenings, some Wednesday afternoons, and on Good Friday evening. The Oberammergau Passion Play, which reconstructs the dramatic events of the last seven days of the Life of Christ, is one of Europe's oldest stage productions. It was presented in this country for the first time in 1932, then became a permanent summertime institution in 1939 when the company settled in an amphitheater in the Black Hills of South Dakota. In 1952 the company opened a second amphitheater just south of Lake Wales.

The Passion Play's cast of 150 is headed by the world famous Christus portrayer, Josef Meier, a German-born American citizen. He is supported by professional actors in all the principal roles. It's an exciting production in a spectacular setting. Tickets cost $4.50, $6, $6.50 and $7 (children under 12 half price). Tickets are are available at the box office, but it's best to make reservations. By mail: Passion Play Amphitheater, Box 71, Lake Wales, FL 33853. By telephone: (813) 676-1495. The amphitheater is located off Route 27A. Because it's an outdoor production, wraps are advisable.

The Way to Go: West on Interstate 4. It's about 27 miles from downtown Orlando to US 27, a right turn on Exit 23. Drive south on 27 for 20 miles to Route 17A (before reaching Lake Wales) and turn left. Continue east and follow signs to Spook Hill in the general direction of Mountain Lake Sanctuary. Roundtrip drive: about two and a half hours.

Tupperware

International headquarters for Tupperware is located south of Orlando near Kissimmee, and while none of the internationally-renowned plastic food and storage containers are manufactured here, it still makes a short, appealing stop.

The main building, designed by the noted architect Edward Durell Stone, blends into a Florida landscape of subtropical gardens and lakes. In the courtyard a beautiful circular fountain—replica of the famous King's Cross Fountain in Sidney, Australia—radiates water 360 degrees. The fountain was presented by Tupperware Australia.

Tours, which last about 30 minutes, are conducted through the exhibit area by charming hostess-demonstrators. Because so many people have shown interest in the manufacturing process of Tupperware, the tour starts with a hostess narrating three-dimensional displays of photographs depicting the step-by-step

At Tupperware's international headquarters near Kissimmee visitors can see the Tupperware manufacturing process and a museum of historic food containers.

procedure of design and engineering; the gathering of materials; production, packaging and distribution.

Tupperware is actually manufactured at a number of overseas works, and in this country in Jerome, Idaho; Halls, Tennessee; Hemingway, South Carolina, and Blackstone, Massachusetts. The 300–400 employees who work at international headquarters outside Orlando are engaged in public relations, advertising, sales, accounting, data processing, etc.

Next stop for visitors is the home exhibition division where the hostesses demonstrate Tupperware products in natural settings of kitchen and breakfast area, patio, dining and living rooms, and a children's section. Yes, Tupperware makes toys too.

Visitors are then invited to spend as much time as they choose in the museums where a collection of historic food containers are housed, the oldest item dating back to 4000 B.C. Containers are grouped into four sections: natural materials, ceramics, metals and glass. More than 100 Tupperware products are displayed in the gallery. The entire museum collection represents the evolution of food containers, and serves as a salute to man's ingenuity and artistry.

Although tours are guided every 25 minutes, Monday through Friday from 9 a.m. to 4 p.m., groups of 20 or more persons should make advance arrangements by phoning (305) 847-3111, extension 2695. There is no admission fee, and each visitor is given a small Tupperware gift as a memento. Also on the grounds is a 2500-seat convention center, where such entertainers as Waylon Jennings, Roger Whittaker and Johnny Mathis have performed.

The Way to Go: South on South Orange Blossom Trail (US 441 and 17-92). The 1,500 acres of Tupperware International overlapping from Orange County into Osceola County, are located six miles south of the Beeline Expressway, and about two miles north of the Kissimmee city limits. Watch for the Tupperware sign on the right side of the highway, but turn left (east) at the first Tupperware driveway.

Brevard Museum, Cocoa Village

Here's a suggestion for a nice little two-stop excursion to Brevard County if you're not planning to go to the beach. Then again, you could stop at Brevard Museum and Cocoa Village on the way to or from the beach.

Brevard Museum won't overwhelm you with its size, but it's a neat building with intriguing exhibits; and recently opened is a little Discovery Room for children, patterned on a similar section of the Smithsonian Institution. Behind the museum are nature trails winding through 22 acres of wilderness. From the top of the hill you suddenly look down on civilization: the sprawling facility of Brevard Community College. A portion of the nature trail is paved for wheelchair traffic.

The non-profit museum has an impressive collection of mounted marine life and shells. Most prominent is the Florida Horse Conch, Florida's official state shell. Permanent exhibits include marine graphic displays, an exotic fish aquarium, Brevard County fossils, Indian artifacts, a reconstructed Brevard hammock, glass boxes of geographic intervals, and more.

You could spend almost an hour just looking through the items in the late 1800s general store.

The Discovery Room, put together by the Junior Service League, is open only from 10 a.m. to 2 p.m., for children from kindergarten age through the sixth grade. There's a working beehive, costumes from foreign countries, fossils, kites from the Smithsonian, books, records, audio-visuals, and discovery boxes the kids can take out to examine and try to identify the contents.

Brevard Museum is closed on Sunday and Monday. Hours Tuesday through Friday: 9 a.m. to 5 p.m.; and 10 a.m. to 4 p.m. on Saturday. Admissions: $1 for adults; 50 cents for children 5–16. Mailing address: Brevard Museum, Inc., 2201 Michigan Avenue, Cocoa, FL 32922. Telephone: (305) 632-1830.

Four miles to the south is Cocoa Village.

Several years ago some civic-conscious citizens and businessmen in Cocoa got together and decided to brighten up a small neighborhood of narrow streets, run-down stores and buildings. This was downtown Cocoa, a semi-ghost town. The renovation was an admirable success, and Cocoa Village was born. What was once lost in the shuffle of commerce and beach-accented tourism is now quite the attraction. Now there's solid reason for cars to turn onto Brevard Avenue from busy Route 520 which shoots over to the ocean.

The restored area is colorful and quaint, a cozy collection of shops and arcades, and the sidewalks and curbs are easily maneuvered by wheelchairs. Browsers and shoppers are coaxed to the open-air mall with gazebo and picnic tables.

You can find books, art galleries, ice cream, souvenirs, gifts, crafts, clocks, clothing, custom carpentry, barber shops, delicatessen, restaurants, and a wonderful toy store which not too long ago was the pride of the more renowned Park Avenue in Winter Park. And the old movie theater is now the stylish Cocoa Village Playhouse for the Performing Arts.

You might not be able to park in front of the business or shop you prefer, but there's sufficient space in a close-by public lot, Taylor Park on Delannoy Avenue and behind the public library. Cocoa Village is delightfully different.

Any questions? Call Cocoa Beach Area Chamber of Commerce at (305) 636-4262. Mailing address: 431 Riveredge Boulevard, Cocoa, FL 32922.

The Way to Go: East on SR 50 (Colonial Drive). Just past Bithlo, bear right on Route 520. Drive about nine miles and turn left on Bee Line Expressway (Route 528 East). Stay on 528 until you reach US 1. Or leave Orlando on the Bee Line (it's a toll road) and travel directly to US 1. Either way, when you come to US 1, turn right and go a mile to Michigan Avenue, turn right again and follow signs for another mile to the museum. It's on the left. To find Cocoa Village, continue south on US 1 from Michigan for four miles to Route 520, turn left. Drive about a half-mile to Brevard Avenue, turn right and you're right there.

Canaveral National Seashore

One of the nation's most precious treasures, positioned midway between Jacksonville and West Palm Beach, is the Canaveral National Seashore—one of the few wilderness areas still left on Florida's Atlantic Coast.

Encompassing nearly 68,000 acres of water and untamed land, it came under governmental protection in January of 1975 when the Seashore was created by Congress. The area, including 25 miles of clean white beaches, stretching from Apollo Beach on the north to Playalinda Beach on the south near the John F. Kennedy Space Center, is open to the public, but the uncompromising emphasis here is on preservation.

The five-mile Playalinda Beach is the most easily accessible tract for visitors. Here, on the eastern flank of the Seashore, you can swim, surf, and surf-fish for Spanish mackerel, whiting, bluefish and many other types of sport fish. Swimmers and surfers should be cognizant, however, of the strong, potentially dangerous ocean currents, and the possibility of encountering a Portuguese man-of-war or one of those pesky, stinging jellyfish. Enter the water only in supervised areas. Lifeguards pull duty at the southern lip of the beach in summer, but only on weekends in the fall and spring.

Tip: The snack bar, just before entering Playalinda, is the only source of supplies inside the Seashore.

The segment of raw beach between Playalinda and Apollo is attractive for hiking, but bear in mind that sun and mosquitoes can be a pain at times, and that there is no fresh drinking water available. Motor vehicles are not allowed on the beach, giving you the unique opportunity of enjoying the environment without intrusion. Also, be aware of rough surf and high tides, both of which can cut down your walking space to little or nothing.

The beaches are banked by high, richly vegetated barrier dunes. On the west side of the Seashore are marshes, tree-packed hammocks ("hammock" is an Indian word meaning "garden-spot"), mangrove stands and that productive subtropical estuary called Mosquito Lagoon.

An incidental note: Mosquito Lagoon is accurately named, which means that if you're away from offshore breezes, it's wise to carry a repellent for protection against mosquitoes and other insects.

Snook, sea trout, redfish, mullet and many more varieties of fish tempt fishermen at Mosquito Lagoon. Less tempting are the alligators. The harmless manatees (sea cows) are often seen here, too.

The Seashore is a haven for a broad assortment of wildlife, some on the list of rare or endangered species. The endangered bald eagle is one example. A few of these diminishing breed take up winter residence in the tall pines. Close to 300 species of birds have been observed in the Seashore and in the neighboring Merritt Island National Wildlife Refuge. A sizable population of brown pelicans, the kind you see gliding gracefully over the beaches, nests in a mangrove island in the center of the Seashore.

The earliest inhabitants on this land, dating back to the time before Christ, were aboriginal Indians. History records the name of Alberto Maxia, a Spaniard, as the first foreign visitor to set foot here. He came from St. Augustine on a scouting mission in 1605.

Canaveral National Seashore is co-managed by the National Park Service and the U.S. Fish & Wildlife Service, Department of the Interior. The Superintendent in personal charge of this area has an office on SR 402, about seven miles east of Titusville on the way to Playalinda: PO Box 2583, Titusville, FL 32780. Telephone (305) 867-4675. Playalinda is occasionally closed when there is special testing or a space shuttle launching at Kennedy Space Center.

Visitors willing to observe the common-sense rules that forbid the disturbing of any of the archeologic sites, find a year-round welcome in the Seashore—but only during daylight hours. There are no fees. Visitors will also find a treasure of life in its natural, primitive, most enchanting condition.

The Way to Go: East on SR 50 to Titusville (40 miles from Orlando). Turn north on US 1 (it runs through the city and parallel with Indian River), and drive about four miles to Route 406. Cross the river here and continue east on Route 402 approximately 10 miles to the beach. Slightly more than halfway from river to beach on 402 is Seashore Headquarters, furnishing restrooms and information. Driving time from Orlando: less than an hour and a half.

Cocoa Beach

Residents of the landlocked Orlando area turn east toward Cocoa Beach in Brevard County for the quickest ride to the ocean. It's as attractive as it is handy, the beach sloping gently into the Atlantic in the shadow of the nation's spaceport, about halfway between Jacksonville and Miami. It gets the stamp of approval from both the older and younger age groups.

Orlando's closest beach is flanked by luxury hotels and motels, apartments and condominiums, lavish and cozy homes, stretching into more isolated regions and then into the Patrick Air Force Base recreation area, just south of the Cocoa Beach city limits. One of the city's more appealing regulations forbids motorized vehicular traffic on the beach.

As you enter town on Route 520, you can drive directly into a beach parking area. There's a 50-cent parking charge. Park-free access streets and driveways can be found down the way, but make sure you don't trespass on private property. Take Route A1A (Atlantic Avenue) south for six miles to the PAFB beach. Although this is federal property, it's open to the public. There are shade trees here, a covered pavilion and a bathhouse. No admission or parking fees.

Cocoa Beach accommodates swimmers, fishermen and surfers, and provides some of the best small-wave surfing conditions in the state. In case you don't carry a surfboard with you, they're available for purchase or rental at just about any of the many surf shops along Atlantic Avenue, including Ron Jon, the biggest and most famous shop of them all, just off the 520-A1A intersection, on the left. Ron Jon is easy to sight because of the tall, ever-changing billboard out front.

The Canaveral Pier, running 825 feet out into the ocean, offers great fishing possibilities. Several surfing tournaments are put on at this location, mostly on Easter and Labor Day weekends. For fishermen, offshore waters yield red snapper, sailfish, snook, drum, redfish, trout and other species. Some folks at the Chamber of Commerce claim that Brevard County is the salt water trout capital of the world. This would include those sparklers taken from the salt water bays of the Indian and Banana Rivers. No license is needed for salt water fishing. If you stray over to the St. Johns River, however, for those fresh water catfish, lunker bass and shad, equip yourself with a license.

Resident and out-of-state fishing licenses may be obtained at any county court house, and just about all the bait and tackle stores, sporting goods stores and fish camps. Or ask a nearby fisherman for the closest location to get a license. Seldom do you come across a body of water in Florida where there is no nearby fisherman.

Write for any information to Cocoa Beach Area Chamber of Commerce, 431 Riveredge Blvd., Cocoa, FL 32922. Telephone: (305) 636-4262.

No trip to Florida is all it should be if you don't at least tip a toe or pole in the ocean.

The Way to Go: East on SR 50 (Colonial Drive) or the toll Bee line Expressway (Route 528 East), to Route 520. This takes you into Cocoa, through Merritt Island and on to Cocoa Beach. About an hour's driving time.

Daytona Beach Museum

No one—certainly not in this book—is advising against a walk, a drive, or a fish-and-swim romp on the "world's most famous beach," that 23-mile sandy strip of the Daytona Beach resort area. There is a museum before arriving at the beach, though, which merits your attention. It is the Museum of Arts & Sciences, and although it's not the world's most famous museum, it is beginning to attract national recognition.

Star of the museum show is a Giant Ground Sloth, a 13-foot-high mounted skeleton, the most complete and best preserved of its species in North America. The mammal migrated from South America and roamed this area 120,000 and 150,000 years ago, and this particular skeleton was discovered several years ago in a shell pit less than three miles from the museum. It was considered a major find of world-wide significance.

The Giant Ground Sloth is part of the permanent exhibits in the Sciences Wing Gallery. There are also rotating science exhibits, and rotating and permanent art exhibits, including the new Cuban Foundation Collection.

The concept of a Cuban Museum in Daytona Beach began in 1952 when the Cuban Foundation was formed. In 1971 the Foundation Collection was placed in the new museum at its present 60-acre site; and, incidentally, was highly instrumental in the drive for more museum space. Finally, in late 1980, the East Wing was opened, the area now housing the Cuban Collection: 150 paintings, carvings, documents, ceramics and furniture, dating from 1759 to 1959, the pre-Castro era.

Other collections: Florida art, American decorative arts, European paintings, 18th and 19th century African art and artifacts, Pleistocene fossils and regional natural history. Because of its close neighbor to the south, the John F. Kennedy Space Center, the museum naturally presents a concentration of space exhibits, information and programs.

The thirteen foot skeleton of a Giant Ground Sloth, one of many fascinating exhibits at the Museum of Arts & Sciences at Daytona Beach. Photo by Mark Losey.

Planetarium programs, such as "The Light Fantastic" and "The Moon—Gateway to the Universe" are shown Wednesday at 7:30 p.m. and Saturday at 2:30 p.m.

The two interpretive nature trails in adjacent Tuscawilla Park take about 20 or 25 minutes to walk.

The museum, a not-for-profit educational institution, chartered by the State of Florida in 1957, and accredited by the American Association of Museums, is open Tuesday through Friday from 9 a.m. to 5 p.m.; Saturday noon until 5 p.m.; and Sunday 1 p.m. to 5 p.m. Closed Monday. Admissions: $1 for adults, 50 cents for children, and $2.50 for families. Free admission on Wednesday afternoon 1 until 5. There are accommodations for wheelchairs.

Mailing address: Museum of Arts & Sciences, 1040 Museum Blvd., Daytona Beach, FL 32014. Telephone: (904) 255-0285.

Based on a recent study, it's apparent that residents of this country now visit museums more frequently than sporting events. The Museum of Arts & Sciences in Daytona Beach is an ideal local example of why this is so.

An additional note: specific information on the communities of Daytona Beach, Daytona Beach Shores, Holly Hill, Ponce Inlet, Ormond Beach, Ormond-by-the-Sea, Port Orange and South Daytona—offering 26,000 hotel and motel rooms, 23 miles of free public beach, exciting nightlife and cultural action—may be obtained by writing The Daytona Beach Resort Area, PO Box 2169, Dept. Y, Daytona Beach, FL 32015.

The Way to Go: East on Interstate 4. Exit on US 92 (which is also Volusia Avenue). Continue east for a few minutes on 92 past Daytona International Speedway and the airport, and turn right on Nova Road (SR 5A). Past the first traffic signal, look on the right for the big green and white Kelly Tires sign, and the smaller brown and white museum sign directing you to South Street, which bends immediately into Museum Boulevard. Keep the canal on your left. It's one of those places you can't miss. In case you do, ask any friendly Daytonan. Driving time: slightly more than an hour.

Daytona
International Speedway

Richard Petty, Bobby Allison, Cale Yarborough, Tiny Lund, David Pearson, Junior Johnson, Buddy Baker, Darrell Waltrip and Fireball Roberts, they all had rides on the Daytona International Speedway—and so can you.

But unless you're a qualified stock car jockey, your ride will be considerably shorter, slower and safer.

Gate No 7 of the banked, 2.5-mile tri-oval race track stays open for visitors who would like to step inside and see what the site of the famous Daytona 500 event looks like; and there is a tour bus standing by to take visitors for a brief spin on the track.

The charge for the bus tour is only $1.00 (children under 12 free), so you can see this is strictly a courtesy service by the track.

But call the track at (904) 253-6711 before making a special excursion here because Gate No. 7 is open to the public only when there are no races, special events or closed tests going on. The Daytona 500 and related speed activities usually monopolize most of February and the first week in March; the Firecracker 400 is July 4, and sports car races are programmed Thanksgiving weekend.

Mailing address: Daytona International Speedway, PO Box S, Daytona Beach, FL 32015.

The Speedway opened in 1959. Before that—long before—headquarters for racing in this part of the world was the sandy slab along the Atlantic coast in Daytona Beach. One of the leading drivers of those yesteryears was Bill France, Sr., president of the Speedway. Today, the Daytona 500-mile race draws an international audience annually in excess of 100,000 persons.

This is the track made famous by Bill France and all those other fearless, floor-boarding drivers of the South, but there were many other crack drivers who didn't fit that good ole boy mold, such as Mark Donohue, Pedro Rodriguez and Mario

Frantic action in the pits during the Daytona 500 stock car race at
Daytona International Speedway.

Andretti—and the roster of names goes on and on. They all had rides here.

And now you?

The Way to Go: East on Interstate 4. Exit on US 92 (which is also Volusia Avenue). Continue east on 92 for a few minutes and watch for the Speedway on the right. It's next to the greyhound racing track and across the highway from the jai-alai fronton. About an hour's driving time.

Fort Christmas Museum

It's conceivable, when dropping in here—depending on the flexibility of one's imagination—to feel closer to the 19th century soldiers and settlers who constructed Fort Christmas than to the inhabitants of present day Orlando only two dozen miles away.

This is not the original fort. The original structure was destroyed by fire years ago, and though there is still unresolved controversy over its exact site, it's generally believed that Fort Christmas was built less than a half-mile to the north near Christmas Creek, on December 25–27, 1837. Regardless, Fort Christmas Museum represents a faithful and artful replica of the type of bulwark used for protection against the Indians during the Second Seminole War (1835–1842).

Inside the tall pine pickets of the fort are a storehouse, a pair of two-story blockhouses, and a powder magazine. It's best to visit the storehouse first where you can sit for a neat audio-visual presentation that puts the geographic and historic facts of the war in perspective. The narration, by the late Bill Berry, a Central Florida radio and television personality, is clear, educational and easy to comprehend.

Inside Blockhouse No. 1 you can see maps, weapons, treaties, uniforms and artifacts of the Seminole Wars, and hear a recorded chant of an Indian medicine man.

The exhibits of Blockhouse No. 2 project an even more intimate and relevant grasp of what it must have been like in the days when sturdy pioneers slashed through the pine forests and cabbage palm hammocks to establish homesteads. Here you can examine a lathing hatchet, broad axe, sugarcane knife, hand sickle, oxen yoke, beehive smoker, palmetto scrub brush, cooking kettle, and other farm equipment, tools and household furnishings. There's also a picture gallery of the first settlers and their descendants.

Across the courtyard you can look into—but not enter—the powder magazine where black powder for the Army's flintlock muskets, and other ammunition, were stored below ground for safety.

Then walk the elevated, hand-railed boardwalk behind the fence and pause at gun ports where soldiers stood guard or fired their weapons. You don't have to be a little boy or girl to peek out through the notched openings and imagine the furtive movements of Indians in the distance.

Fort Christmas was erected by the 3rd Regiment of Artillery, four companies of the 3rd and 4th Dragoons, and four companies of Alabama Volunteers—most likely with assistance from the settlers. Then, when the soldiers pushed along to other battlefronts, a number of civilian families stayed in the area, and they too took the name of Fort Christmas for their community. The "Fort" was dropped from the name of the settlement when the United States government opened a post office in 1892.

The museum was built by the Orange County Parks Department, and dedicated in December of 1977 to the soldiers, Indians, slaves and pioneers—rugged Americans all—who lived and died on this defiant land a century and a half ago. Museum hours: 10 a.m. to 5 p.m., Tuesday through Saturday; 1 p.m. to 5 p.m. Sunday; closed Monday and all county holidays. In the park outside the fort: picnic tables, playgrounds, restrooms. Everything's free.

The Way to Go: East on SR 50. After entering Christmas (look only for the sign because there are no other landmarks), turn

Fort Christmas Museum, site of a stronghold for soldiers and settlers during the Second Seminole War (1835-1842). Photo by Dennis Wall.

left on Ft. Christmas Road (Orange County 420). It's two more miles to the museum.

* * *

Before leaving the small unincorporated town of Christmas, don't forget to drop your cards and letters in the mailbox for that unique postmark. The Christmas, Florida (32709) Post Office—it's the little brown building with holiday wreaths in the windows and oversized greeting cards planted in the yard—is on SR 50. As you return from the museum on Ft. Christmas Road, turn left on 50. Drive slowly and look hard to the right for the post office or you'll miss it.

* * *

Hermon Brooks, celebrated hunter, adventurer and alligator breeder, picks up his mail at the Christmas Post Office. He lives three miles farther east on SR 50 on a spread called Gator Jungle. He and his wife Annette and their teenaged sons, Shane and Wayne, run the low-key attraction that features wildlife (just about every kind you can find in Florida), and a covered bridge spanning a body of water swarming with gators. There's a small admission fee here ($2 for adults and $1 for children 3 and up), but it's worth it. Telephone: (305) 568-2885. The Brooks family keeps the place open every day from 9 a.m. until dark. Drive slowly and look hard to the left or you'll miss it.

Kennedy Space Center

On this land, 45 miles east of Orlando, the United States rocketed a man into space for the first time; lifted a man to the moon; and today the property serves as the primary launch and landing site for the space shuttle, a manned reusable space vehicle which takes off like a rocket and returns to earth like a jetliner.

This is the National Aeronautics and Space Administration's John F. Kennedy Space Center. Even though the center itself falls into the category of a big Florida attraction, it's possible to spend several entertaining and informative hours at the visitors center without the necessity of spending a cent. Admission is free and it's open every day except Christmas, 8 a.m. to dark.

Anyone determined to take a closer look at the innards of Kennedy Space Center—to view present and past launch sites, an authentic Apollo/Saturn V space vehicle, and the gargantuan vehicle assembly building—should take one of the conducted bus tours. They run from the visitors center until two hours before dark. The cost is reasonable. While tours are conducted in English, foreign language tapes are provided for 25 or more adults if advance arrangements are made. For these, and for big group reservations, call (305) 452-2121. Or write KSC Tours, Visitors Center, TWA 810, Kennedy Space Center, FL 32899.

From the time NASA was formed in 1958, more than 300 launches have been handled by Kennedy Space Center. Remember the blaze of Mercury and Gemini, and the thunder of Apollo, Skylab and Gemini? All those missions took place right here. And blastoffs of unmanned spacecrafts continue periodically: weather and communications satellites, earth resources technological satellites, orbiting scientific observatories, etc., both for this country and for other governments.

Want to see a blastoff? When you're in Florida you can call (800) 432-2153 for toll-free information and dates of upcoming launchings.

In the beginning NASA might have been regarded as an agency strictly out to win a space race with Russia, but it was a good deal more than that; and infinitely more comprehensive now. Even in its early stages, data from instrumented satellites led to the discovery of the Van Allen radiation belt, helped perceive the shape of the earth's magnetic field and earth itself, and supplied counts and density measurements of particles in space. Mariner, Pioneer, Viking and Voyager space vehicles collect facts about neighboring planets and interplanetary space.

Satellites have brought back information about the sun; solar flares and wind; and the relationship of sun cycles to events on our planet; mounting information that expands our understanding of how weather is affected by cycles of activity on the sun, and how magnetic space storms influence or meddle with communications on earth.

It's taken man a long time to get into space and to concoct that first almost unbelievably successful moonshot. The entire world held its breath as Neil Armstrong prepared to take a walk on the moon, but now the constant flow of aerospace triumphs are taken for granted. Perhaps it's because our minds can't absorb it all as man reaches deeper and deeper into the riddles of space, as scientists seem to be outstepping the writer of science fiction.

Yet, all mankind stands to benefit from what's afoot here in Florida. As just one example, the fabulously successful and little publicized LANDSAT series of satellites furnishes a running overview of earth and events taking place down below, probing the likes of water and industrial pollution, soil erosion and crop diseases, defining petroleum provinces in upper Alaska and mineral deposits in other countries.

Kennedy Space Center is yesterday, today and tomorrow.

The glamour object of tomorrow is the space shuttle. One of the several free films at the visitors center gives an easy-to-understand explanation of the space shuttle, an aerospace vehicle designed to carry heavy pay loads into earth orbit, and with each orbiter manufactured for reuse, perhaps as often as 100 times. At present the shuttle's maximum altitude, with seven persons aboard, is 1,000 kilometers, or about 600 miles. Typical missions on east-west orbits are programmed to last from a week to a month, taking off from—and landing at—Kennedy Space Center. NASA expects to be launching shuttles on north-south orbital flights from Vandenberg Air Force Base in California by the middle 1980s.

Also at the visitors center you find exhibits galore, indoors and outdoors: the Lunar roving vehicle, Apollo space suit, Lunar module trainer, Saturn V F-1 engine, a "garden" of rockets, all kinds of models, an Apollo 17 moon rock, and so on. It's O.K. to use your camera at the visitors center, or on one of the two-hour guided bus tours of KSC and Cape Canaveral Air Force Station. There are gift and snack shops, the Carousel Cafeteria, and free use of dog kennels.

Enjoy yourself. Excite yourself. Enlighten yourself. Whether you're an American or not, you'll surely flush with pride at man's attainments.

The Way to Go: East on SR 50 (Colonial Drive). From downtown Orlando you can take the East-West Expressway (toll road but a good investment) to eliminate about five miles of heavy traffic. Expressway turns into and ends at SR 50. Drive directly toward Titusville, and take Route 405 East to the first Kennedy Space Center gate. Continue another six miles (you'll cross the Intracoastal Waterway bridge and enter Merritt Island National Wildlife Refuge), then turn right at the visitors center sign. Roundtrip: about 90 miles.

Merritt Island National Wildlife Refuge

Twenty years ago, Kennedy Space Center was founded on a segment of Merritt Island in Brevard County. Because all the land was not required as space program work space, it was decided to mark off some of the property and establish the Merritt Island National Wildlife Refuge. Motive: preserve this primitive, natural, historic environment; provide and protect a sanctuary for wintering waterfowl and the island's many permanent residents of the bird and animal world, and open to the public a managed recreational area.

The refuge lies under the Atlantic Flyway. This is a major, 4,000-mile route for birds winging from their breedings in

Canada and Alaska to Merritt Island. It's estimated that nearly 200,000 ducks and coots drop in here in the fall and winter. Others fly farther south to the Caribbean.

The refuge is more than a sanctum for these birds, of course, as you can find out for yourself on the hiking trail and the two motor drives. Come to Merritt Island National Wildlife Refuge Headquarters for detailed information and how to best spend your time here. The building is located about five and a half miles east of Indian River, on the southside of SR 402.

You can drive through pine flatwoods and along marshes to observe waterfowl, wading birds, alligators and occasionally a few other critters like the bobcat, raccoon, rabbit and armadillo. Birdlife enthusiasts have counted close to 300 bird species on the island, including the bald eagle. Some of the showier winged characters are herons, egrets, seagulls, osprey, brown pelicans (some white pelicans in winter) and spoonbills.

Early morning and late afternoon are the proven times to observe wildlife in its most active state. If you're intent on making both drives, and hiking the Oak Hammock Trail (an interesting nature walk), plan to spend at least two hours.

Inside these boundaries you might find it difficult to believe you're only minutes away from the pad where the United States shot men to the moon. You're actually within short walking distance (if such a walk were permitted) of the space shuttle landing strip. An intriguing, mixed picture.

It might disturb some people that the hunting of migratory waterfowl is permissible on the island in the fall, but it's a traditional—even vital—recreation which is carefully controlled. At refuge headquarters you can obtain all the regulations on the use of firearms (and possibly a few words of hunting philosophy). Fish & Wildlife Service, National Park Service, and NASA are the governmental agencies entrusted with management of the refuge.

Written information may be obtained from the manager, Merritt Island National Wildlife Refuge, PO Box 6504, Titusville, FL 32780. Telephone: (305) 867-4820.

The refuge is open only during the day. No admission charge.

The Way to Go: East on SR 50 to Titusville (40 miles from Orlando). Turn north on US 1 (it crosses through the eastern rim of the city, parallel with Indian River), and drive about four miles to Route 406. Cross the river here and continue east on Route 402 about five and a half miles to refuge headquarters. Driving time is less than an hour and a half.

New Smyrna Sugar Mill Ruins

Four miles to the west of New Smyrna Beach's ocean-front homes and condominiums stand the ghostly remains of an early 19th century sugar mill. Despite the appointment as a state historic site, these ruins are bypassed by too many visitors as they speed to and from their adventures in swimming, sunbathing, fishing and surfing along the magnetic Atlantic coastline. New Smyrna Sugar Mill Ruins is an unfading reminder of the struggle for survival in the early chapters of American history.

Production of sugar and molasses was no snap enterprise on the frontier, and while the industry flourished only briefly (roughly from 1821 to 1835) it did attract new life to an untamed region. And it was here that the Indians initiated their first big-scale attack of the prolonged Second Seminole War.

As history reveals, many of the Seminoles preferred a renegade's risky freedom over deportation to reservations in Oklahoma. Thus, in late December of 1835, a band of about 100 Indians attacked the sugar mill here, corraled the slaves and cattle for their own benefit, forced the occupants to flee, and set fire to the mill and all the plantation buildings. Today, only a portion of the mill's time-beaten walls of coquina rock and a few pieces of equipment remain.

From New Smyrna, those marauding Seminoles continued their rape of approximately 15 other sugar plantations up the coast, from Mosquito Inlet (now Ponce Inlet) to near St. Augustine. Less than a month into the new year they had managed to wipe out the entire sugar industry in this part of the world—evidently forever.

Sugarcane was usually planted in midwinter and harvested the next fall. Stalks were laboriously hand cut, loaded into wagons and hauled to the mill. Its juices were extracted by feeding the stalks into heavy iron rollers, powered by steam, and the juice was piped into the kettle room where it was slowly heated in huge iron kettles and reduced to thick syrup. The syrup was then poured into wooden cooling vats, and that's where it crystallized into granular sugar.

Dark and wet at this point, the sugar was packed into hogshead barrels and left in the curing house from three to four weeks. During this period, molasses, a precious byproduct, oozed from the barrel seams and filled a cistern beneath the curing house floor. When both products were ready for shipping, they were carted to Mosquito Lagoon and loaded aboard schooners, the sugar ticketed for the lively port towns of St. Augustine, Jacksonville and Savannah, the molasses bound for the Bahamas for use in the production of rum.

When visiting New Smyrna Sugar Mill Ruins, located in a pretty, tree-shaded park, you can get a graphic concept of the old step-by-step process of sugar making, although your imagination will have to furnish the product itself. Examine the coquina-block foundation, walls and archways; and walk the pine needle-matted nature trail behind the mill.

Picknicking is not permitted in this park. Restroom facilities are provided. The historic ruins are open daily from 9 a.m. to 5 p.m. No admission charge. Mailing address: New Smyrna Sugar Mill Ruins State Historic Site, PO Box 861, New Smyrna Beach, FL 32069. Telephone: (904) 428-2126.

The Way to Go: East on Interstate 4 to the DeLand-New Smyrna Beach exit (35 miles from downtown Orlando). East on Route 44 approximately 17 miles, turn right at Mission Road and drive another mile to the gate of the ruins. Driving time: an hour and fifteen minutes.

Sebastian Inlet

Pirates struck here in 1719. They struck again in 1980. Well, actually, the modern-day pirates were more like burglars. In fact, they *were* burglars.

Let's start at the beginning.

In the summer of 1715, a dozen galleons, heavy with people and treasures of gold and silver, were sailing from Mexico and Peru off the coast of Florida, homeward bound for Spain. Slowly, menacingly, they were tracked by a monster of a storm from the south. The great ships tossed and turned on the enraged Atlantic like toy sailboats; the sun was erased by clouds; and suddenly the skies were black all around. Wind-driven rain punished the fleet with a force the passengers had never before seen. They were trapped by a hurricane!

There are only estimates of how many galleons rode out the storm, but a number of them sank to the bottom of the sea, and 1,500 men, women and children managed to get ashore from the wrecks, reaching land that is today designated as Sebastian Inlet State Recreation Area.

When word of the hurricane's disaster reached government officials at St. Augustine (about 150 miles to the north), Indians were dispatched to help survivors set up a camp. In a territory of mosquitoes, alligators, sand dunes and mango swamps backed by tropical hammock, it was a deleterious existence at best, and many people died. Those who persisted did manage in time to salvage various loads of the sunken treasures, but later an English pirate named Henry James raided the camp and sailed off with the gold and silver.

A portion of the precious cargoes remained on the ocean floor, however, and it was not until 1963 that an American underseas exploration mission recovered pieces of it. A small cache of the recovery, gold and silver coins worth an estimated $250,000, was encased in glass and placed on exhibition at McLarty Museum, located in the recreation area.

Then, in February of 1980, burglars broke into the museum at night and made off with the treasure. Authorities eventually recovered it, but as of this writing the state has not yet replaced the historic riches in the exhibition room of the museum. That's unfortunate. The missing coins rob the room of a glamorous centerpiece; and yet, the museum is still worth a visit.

Located about midway between Melbourne to the north and Vero Beach to the south, at the southernmost tip of the recreation area, the museum was constructed at the shipwreck salvage site on coastal property which had been deeded to the state by an Atlanta attorney, Robert McLarty. The museum displays articles used by the Ais Indians (believed to be the first inhabitants of the region), other historic and geographic arti- facts, exhibits of marine archeology, and a most interesting diorama showing what the shipwreck survivors' camp must have looked like more than two and a half centuries ago. Periodically, park rangers conduct a slide-tape presentation, a compelling and illuminating glimpse of nature in this part of the world that also signals a sharp warning about soil erosion and man's impatient infringement on the environment.

The museum is closed on Monday and Tuesday. It's open the rest of the week, including Sunday, from 9 to 12 in the morning and 1 to 5 in the afternoon. Admission is 50 cents. No charge for children. Despite the closeness of McLarty Museum (a few minutes' drive past Sebastian Inlet), it's visited by only a fraction of the people who make use of the area. Really, everyone should inspect the museum at least once.

The 576 acres of Sebastian Inlet State Recreation Area (less than a mile wide) are situated on a barrier island, divided by a man-made inlet that links Indian River with the Atlantic Ocean. The lagoon, flanked by dunes, hammock and swamp, is one of the most productive marine habitats on earth. Birdlife teems. There are overnight camping facilities for recreational vehicles, but reservations should be made 60 days in advance. Write Sebastian Inlet State Recreation Area, PO Box 728, Wabasso, FL 32970. Or telephone (305) 589-3754. Overnight fee is $5.20, or $7.28 for electrical hookup.

Motorists have a flashy view of the ocean and inlet from the north-south highway bridge on Route A1A, but the beauty is deceptive. The water of the inlet on the ocean side is ominous, choppy and exceedingly dangerous even in placid weather. The inlet has a grim history of people drowning and boats capsizing. Here's some plain, good old-fashioned advice: stay out of the current-tangled inlet.

A sturdy stone jetty angles out into the ocean, and serves as a popular platform for fishermen and onlookers. In winter months especially there's a good chance you'll feel the spray of the ocean out here. Licenses are not required for salt water fishing. There is also fishing from the beach on the north side of the jetty, suitable swimming conditions, some of the best surfing waves in Florida, and a store that sells provisions.

No charges of any kind for day visitors.

The Way to Go: SR 50 east to Interstate 95. Travel south on the interstate (toward Miami) and get off on the Melbourne, Route 192 exit. Drive east into Melbourne, cross US 1 and the Intracoastal Waterway, then turn south on Route A1A and drive less than 20 miles to Sebastian Inlet. Or south on US 441 out of Orlando. This carries you through Kissimmee and past St. Cloud. Take Route 192 East at Holopaw to Interstate 95, and follow same instructions as above. Time: less than two hours.

Shrimping

Because of its abounding lakes, creeks, rivers and assorted waterways—not to mention the ocean—Central Florida is an authentic paradise for fishermen. Any chamber of commerce will tell you that. And when they tell it, believe 'em hook, line 'n sinker. Weather conditions, naturally, play a big part, and you can hear all about this and the can't-miss sites from any of the hundreds of fish camps, sporting goods stores and bait shops in the locality.

If you're looking for something different, though, why not try shrimping?

It is a seasonal enterprise, best in the fall, or in the spring if not too cold. Shrimp go to sea to spawn in the summer.

The most productive place for the netting of shrimp in our slice of Florida is the Intracoastal Waterway at Oak Hill, just off US 1, between Titusville and New Smyrna Beach. You can launch or rent a boat at one of the fish camps. Launch and rental fees vary. You'll need your own equipment: a long-handled net, container, and, because it's strictly a nocturnal recreation, a light.

The following information is based on experience: shrimp usually start running late in October and early in November, they begin to peak in February, and could stay heavy through late April. The most fertile time to drop your net is the week before, during, and just after the full moon. High, outgoing tide is best. *The Orlando Sentinel* provides a daily table of ocean tides in the sports section under the Page 2 Scoreboard. Look for *low* tides at Daytona Beach. It'll be just the opposite at Oak Hill. As an example, say low tide is midnight at Daytona Beach. This means midnight will be high tide at Oak Hill, and the best time to go shrimping. There are two high tides and two low tides in the daily oceanic cycle. The *Today* newspaper in Cocoa and the *Daytona Beach News Journal* also publish daily tide tables, but remember that high winds affect tides, so the predictions are not infallible.

No license is required for sport shrimping, but Volusia County imposes a limit of five gallons of shrimp per boat. Which, incidentally, is quite a mess of shrimp. For information and conditions, check with Bud Dewees or his son Mark at Lefils Camp: (904) 345-3300.

You can also shrimp off the Titusville Memorial Pier—nets and lights may be rented here—although yields have not been so bountiful. The pier is in Brevard County where there is no limit on catches. However, to discourage the taking of small catches, shrimp should not exceed 47 per pound, or 70 shrimps with head removed per pound. The pier telephone: (305) 267-7720. There are no facilities for the shipping of your shrimp catches.

The Way to Go: East on SR 50. Turn left (north) on US 1 at Titusville. Orlando to Oak Hill round trip: about 110 miles.

Tosohatchee
State Preserve

Controversy is one of the best advertising tools, and you need look no farther than the Tosohatchee State Preserve in Orange County for proof.

Since 1977 when the State of Florida purchased this wooded stronghold of 28,000 acres from 39 private owners under the environmentally endangered land program, it has been maintained by the Department of Natural Resources as a game preserve and park. Yet, it wasn't until the first month of 1981 that many people—Orange Countians included—took notice of its existence.

Avid hunters and zealous environmentalists knew it was there all right, and periodically they publicly argued over rights, but when the state sanctioned an 18-day hunt within its untamed boundaries, that was the shot heard round the county and across Florida. The arguments burst into court and headlines. Suddenly everyone wanted to know just exactly where this preserve was hidden.

According to parks division records, fewer than 1,500 persons in 1980 paid a visit to the Tosohatchee Preserve, located about 25 miles east of Orlando. The small visitor total looks even skimpier when weighed against its annual upkeep cost of $1 million, and when compared to the 90,000 men, women and children who daily attend—in peak season—Walt Disney World at the opposite end of the county.

A check of records, though, covering a six-month span late in 1984 and lapping over into 1985, shows a sizable jump of visitors to Tosohatchee, something like a 50 percent increase compared to the same months of previous years.

At the same time—at this writing, at least—the hunt-minded Florida Game & Fresh Water Commission and the Florida Wildlife Federation seem to be at peace with the Audubon Society, which prefers to keep every inch of the preserve unspoiled and every creature unmolested.

"Right now everything is real smooth," says Capt. Azell G. Nail of the Bureau of Environmental Land Management.

Currently, 23 days of quota hunting are permitted in October, November and December—on staggered weekends. Park rangers open the property to the public every day at 8 a.m., and close at sundown. There is no admission charge.

Those with no eye for natural beauty or feel for ecology might visit here and wonder what all the hullabaloo is about. There are no concession stands, souvenirs, rides or commercial huckstering. No waiting lines either. It's primitive Florida. It's jungle, throttled by wax myrtle and cabbage palm. It's 14,000 acres of pine flatwoods and 3,000 acres of cypress trees, some a century old. Tosohatchee is deer, rabbits, raccoons, armadillos, quail, eagles, egrets, ospreys, turkeys, bobcats, skunks and big fox squirrels.

But there is also a Tosohatchee Ranch House, an outpost built of cedar in 1916 and being converted into a visitors center with historic exhibits. The land in this region was a battlefield during the Second Seminole War (see Fort Christmas Museum). There's a 15-mile scenic drive, picnic grounds and a meandering boardwalk through the wilds and across swamps, and 38 miles of horseback riding trails. Those wishing to use the preserve's limited campsites must call in advance, (305) 568-5893. Bring your own water and equipment. There are 22 miles of backpacking trails, but at present they're not as clearly defined or worked as those in other areas of the state (see Ocala National Forest).

Man has put his marks on the Tosohatchee, but it's still crude. Appropriately so. That's the adventure of it.

The Way to Go: East on SR 50 to Christmas. Turn right on Taylor Creek Road. Watch for the entrance to the Tosohatchee Preserve on the left a few miles farther along. Another way, and this might be best through 1985 because of a bridge rebuilding: East on SR 50 past Bithlo to SR 520, go east about 5 miles to Taylor Creek Road, turn left and drive about another 3 miles.

Turtle Mound

A garbage dump preserved as a state historical memorial?

That's right—although the Indians responsible for the mound would hardly recognize it today.

Turtle Mound covers two acres of land at the northern tip of what is now known as the Canaveral National Seashore. The mound, rising approximately 40 feet, was created by the Surreque Indians after 600 years of oyster feasting. They collected the oysters from Mosquito Lagoon, and after their meals, this is where they discarded the shells. But it became more than a garbage dump. In time the pile of shells offered a vantage point where the tribes could see in all directions and watch for enemy invaders. Visible from 15 miles at sea, it also served as an important landmark, and appeared on 16th century maps.

Today, Turtle Mound is overspread with tropical and subtropical vegetation, although the oyster shells are still very much in evidence.

Visitors are invited to climb the mound. The boardwalk and handrails make it a much easier climb than when the Indians roamed the region from 600 to 1200 AD. However, the angle is rather steep and not recommended for wheelchairs. At the foot of the trail, help yourself to one of the little booklets, designed to add perspective to your trek. The various numbered stations along the way up are explained in the booklet, detailing the types of plants, trees, insects and animals you're apt to sight in this lush little forest. A cabbage palm, a wild orange tree, torchwood, wild coffee, inkwood, lizards, rabbits and raccoons, and an abundance of butterflies in warm weather, all this and more contribute to the daily scenario of nature at work and play.

At the summit of the mound there's an illusion of being much higher than you are—because of the flatness of the surrounding landscape. It's easy enough to stand on either the north or south tower and imagine an Indian at your side sharing the view.

A number of smaller shell heaps were dispersed throughout the New Smyrna Beach area, about 20 or so, but they have been destroyed, and some used for roadbed material. Turtle Mound, so named in 1823, was preserved when purchased in 1924 by the Florida State Historical Society for $8,000. Formerly managed as Turtle Mound State Archeological Site, it now is part of Canaveral National Seashore: PO Box 2583, Titusville, FL 32780. Telephone (305) 867-4675.

Turtle Mound is always open during daylight hours. No admission fee.

The Way to Go: East on Interstate 4 to the DeLand-New Smyrna Beach exit (35 miles from downtown Orlando). East on Route 44 into New Smyrna Beach. Turn left toward the business district on Canal Street. You might want to stop at the New Smyrna Beach/Edgewater Chamber of Commerce office at 115 Canal—on the left side of the main drag, just before the waterfront—to load up on more information about the area. A block to the north you can cross the bridge over the Intracoastal Waterway (it's a drawbridge), and then the Atlantic beach is just two miles away. Atlantic Avenue is the first thoroughfare running parallel with the beach. It cuts into A1A. Turtle Mound is 10 miles south of New Smyrna Beach on A1A. Just when you think you've about run out of road, you're there. Roundtrip: about 130 miles.

Dade Battlefield

January 1, 1836 was the deadline decreed by the United States Government for the exodus of the Seminole Indians from Florida to reservations in Oklahoma. Aware of the Seminoles' untoward reaction to this order, and sensing possible resistance to the move, the military command at Fort Brooke (now Tampa) decided to dispatch reinforcements to the garrison at Fort King (Ocala), about 90 miles to the east, where the Indian agency was located.

On the first three days of the march out of Fort Brooke, the 108 reinforcements, led by Major Francis L. Dade, were kept under furtive surveillance by the Indians. In the early morning of December 28, 1835, the soldiers approached a substantial breadth of open territory, and for awhile at least concentrated vigilance seemed unnecessary; and so the flanking scouts were pulled in.

The men clumped along in sullen silence, two-thirds of the march now behind them. The day was cold.

Suddenly, at about 8 a.m., the Indians attacked the unsuspecting soldiers, firing point blank from behind the longleaf pines and thick palmettos. Up and down the line men fell to the ground, many before they had a chance to un-shoulder their rifles. Major Dade was killed almost instantly. In a short time half his command lay wounded or dead.

This ambush, now emblazoned in American history as the Dade Massacre, was the incident that touched off the Second Seminole War, a conflict that would drag out seven years and become the country's costliest Indian war ever.

Those soldiers who survived the opening onslaught of the Seminoles were finally able to return some rifle fire and maneuver their lone small cannon into position to unload several shots. At this the Indians withdrew temporarily, allowing the soldiers time to try regrouping, administer to their wounded and swiftly erect a low breastwork of logs. Disoriented, outnumbered and outfoxed, the soldiers were easy prey as the enemy launched its second assault.

At last, about 2 p.m., the final shot was heard. Dade's command had been practically wiped out. The Indians, supported by runaway slaves, moved in, killed the wounded, pillaged the bodies and supplies, dumped the cannon into a water hole and fled. Somehow, three soldiers managed to escape; however, some sources believe that only one of the three was able to get all the way back to Fort Brooke to give a detailed recounting of the ghastly bushwhacking.

It wasn't until February 20, 1836 that an expedition reached the scene of the ambush to bury the dead with military rites. The cannon was retrieved and mounted, its muzzle turned down as a memorial to the dead. In 1842, U.S. Army officers and men pitched in to help pay for the final interment of Dade's Command in the National Cemetery at St. Augustine.

The State of Florida has designated Dade Battlefield, just outside the city of Bushnell in Sumter County, an official state historic site. This is the exact site where the Dade Massacre occurred a century and a half ago. You're invited to walk a portion of the infamous Fort King Military Road; read the markers along the nature trail in the pine forest; try to get a pulse on what took place as the 108 soldiers trudged along on that chilly December morn in Florida, each with his own thoughts and hopes.

There's also a small museum to add a stark vein of realism: audio tape, exhibits and artifacts. Across the road from the museum is a log breastwork of the type the soldiers quickly put together for protection against the Indians.

An admission fee of 25 cents is charged museum visitors 5 years of age and over. Guided group tours available; make arrangements in advance. Write: Dade Battlefield Historic Site, PO Box 938, Bushnell, FL 33513. Telephone: (904) 793-4781. The battlefield site, picnic area and museum are open every day from 8 a.m. to 5 p.m., holidays included.

The Way to Go: West on SR 50 for 39 miles, then turn right on Route 469. The highway becomes Route 48 in Center Hill. Stay on 48 through the hamlet of Bevilles Corner into Bushnell. Watch for the Dade Battlefield sign. From Orlando it's about an hour and a half drive.

Florida Citrus Tower

Yes, there are hills in Central Florida—rolling hills—and you can best see them from the Florida Citrus Tower in Clermont. With a view of 2,000 square miles, it's billed as the highest point in the state.

Ride the elevator to the open or enclosed platforms of the 200-foot tower, and take in the panorama of rolling green, the spring-fed lakes, and—count 'em!—17 million citrus trees. Well you don't have to count 'em. Take our word for it.

Spectacular—that's easily the best word to describe this view.

Angling off from the base of the tower are a restaurant and a motel; a glass workshop where you can watch nationally known artists designing delicate pieces of fine lead crystal; an ice cream patio and a candy kitchen that feature countless flavors, including citrus; a packing house where you can select your own fruit to buy or have shipped; and an international gift shop.

This complex is worth a special trip, and especially makes a great stop on the way to or from one of the other nearby locales described in these pages. Admissions to the tower are within reason: $1.50 for adults, $1 for the 10–15 age group, and rides are free for boys and girls under 10. And you can stay atop the tower for as long as you like (or at least until the 6 p.m. closing). Restaurant opens at 7 a.m., closes at 3 p.m. That's every day. Phone: (904) 394-2145.

The Way to go: West on SR 50 to Clermont, one mile north or US 27. From downtown Orlando or Interstate 4, drive west on the East-West Expressway (toll road). It joins SR 50. About a 30-minute drive.

Florida
Southern College

For a moment, forget that Florida Southern College is a much-respected, four-year, liberal arts, co-educational house of learning founded in 1885 by the Methodist Church. Of more interest to the campus visitor with no educational or emotional ties here: Florida Southern College represents the biggest concentration of Frank Lloyd Wright architecture in the world.

If it were not for the non-conformist, creative brilliance of Frank Lloyd Wright, this institution would probably be just another pretty face along Florida's orange-grove, lakeside colleges. As it is—located on Lake Hollingsworth in Lakeland, about 55 miles west of Orlando—Florida Southern College is known worldwide.

The school, maintaining a capacity enrollment of approximately 1,600 students, invites visitors throughout the year to take walking tours of the campus, enjoy the restful atmosphere, and examine the buildings designed and structurally supervised by the poetic architect; and to further inspect the newer additions with the Wright brand as carried out by his protegé, Nils Schweizer. Wright died in 1959.

Architecturally, Florida Southern stands today as the fulfillment of a dream—the dream of an ultramodern campus born in the imagination of the late Dr. Ludd M. Spivey, a Methodist minister and president of the school from 1925 to 1957. Dr. Spivey apparently was inspired by a war memorial he visited in Europe, and after reading the autobiography of Wright in 1936, he visited the world's most famous architect at his Wisconsin hideaway in Taliesin East at Spring Green.

Dr. Spivey presented this proposition to Wright: "I have no money with which to build this modern American campus, but if you'll design the buildings, I'll work night and day to raise the means."

Wright, 67 at the time, visited the 100-acre campus, and in the next two decades, seven of his unconventional, stunning buildings would emerge from the sand and groves on the west campus, everlastingly reaching for the sun, forming what he would later label "the only true American campus." During this time Wright became a familiar, jaunty, sometimes haughty figure around Lakeland in his flowing cape and walking stick, his head covered with either beret or pork-pie hat.

His first building, the Annie Pfeiffer Chapel (dedicated in 1941, three years after the cornerstone was laid), did not meet with instant huzzahs from observers. With its unusual "steeple" designed to sift in sunlight from various angles, and standing alone, it looked something like a medieval fortress. But this was just the beginning of the master plan of 18 units, patterned "as the cultural value of organic buildings well suited to time, purpose and place."

Florida Southern College in Lakeland is known worldwide for the beauty of its campus architecture, which was designed by Frank Lloyd Wright.

Even so, a few years later, American Architects chose the chapel as one of the most beautiful buildings in the United States.

Wright's basic building materials were steel for strength, mixed with Florida sand and glass "to bring God's outdoors into man's indoors." The concrete blocks were designed by Wright and made on campus. ("They will be standing a thousand years into the future," Wright promised.)

There were steel and manpower shortages during the 1940 wartime years as the unique circular library went up, but construction proceeded as many of the students—male and female—pitched in as laborers. Dedicated in 1945, the library is currently used as an office building. The much larger Roux Library was constructed in 1966.

Wright also introduced the esplanade to the American college campus, the classic portico, a sheltered promenade connecting the west campus buildings and forming the quadrangle. The three-level Polk Science Building, containing one of Central Florida's few planetariums, was the last of the Wright structures to be completed (1958). Cost: $1 million plus.

"Florida Southern College may never be more than just a freshwater college among the big institutions of the country, but its architecture will cause it to become a beacon of light," Wright proudly predicted.

He also observed: "This type of architecture can't mean much to you until you have a good look at yourself. This architecture represents the laws of harmony and rhythm . . .

"College buildings today are hangovers from an architecture that for 500 years tended to make people feel inferior. The function of architecture, and it's going to be the function of education, is to stress the beautiful."

In addition to establishing itself as an educational institution of quality and distinction, Florida Southern has exceptional programs in the performing arts, and in intramural and inter-scholastic athletics. The Moccasin baseball team has hoisted four national titles, and the basketball team earned a No. 1 national ranking. The Polk County school is affiliated with the Florida Conference of The United Methodist Church, and has a proficient public relations department that responds swiftly to written or in-person inquiries. Mailing address: Lakeland, FL 33802. Telephone: (813) 683-5521.

Dr. Spivey commissioned Frank Lloyd Wright to plant greatness here. Come see it.

The Way to Go: West on Interstate 4, and turn right off the US 98 exit. Stay on 98 until you reach Memorial Boulevard. Turn left and drive to Ingraham Avenue. Turn right and stay on Ingraham until reaching the campus. Allow yourself a little more than an hour of driving time from Orlando to campus.

Rogers' Christmas House

It's like tiptoeing into fairyland.

And when you leave, it's almost impossible not to take with you the warm feeling of peace and good will.

Yule—shimmeringly pure and simple—is the perpetual setting in the original Rogers' Christmas House & Village in Brooksville. Calling this a gift shop does it no justice at all. It's a commercial enterprise, of course, yet one can say that in the nicest sense. It's worth a visit even if you have no intention of buying as much as a greeting card. Browsers are as welcome as buyers.

The ten rooms of Christmas House are sprinkled with tinkling music, and bedecked with all the charm of an old-fashioned holiday season: hundreds of exquisite imported and domestic lights, and countless Christmas trees, wreaths, ornaments and arrangements. There are gifts and gift ideas for all ages and all seasons, including the broadest selection of ornaments in the country, and those in-demand, limited edition Christmas Commemoratives, all crafted by experts.

There's more.

There's the Little House Under the Oak Tree, the Brides House, Storybook Land with animated figures, and Christmas

Cottage, all adjoining the original House, all loaded with graceful home and decorating accessories and gifts.

Christmas House & Village is open every day of the year except Christmas Day (even St. Nick needs a holiday). No matter the season, hours are always the same: 9:30 a.m. to 5 p.m., Monday through Saturday; and 10:30 a.m. to 5 p.m. on Sunday. Telephone: (904) 796-2415.

The Way to Go: It's a straight run of 65 miles west on SR 50. Christmas House is located one block from the convergence of US 90 and US 41. As you enter Brooksville, turn right one block before reaching the first stoplight.

Saint Leo
College

Bedded down in the hilly greenery of Pasco County, the tiny town of Saint Leo is basically an educational and religious community, although its boundaries do encompass some other private property. The town is unincorporated, has its own mayor (at present a lay woman), and its own ZIP code.

You're not permitted in Saint Leo Abbey where 30 monks reside, or in Holy Name Priory with its 30 nuns in residence; but aside from the monastery and the convent, visitors are welcome to come experience the softness and tranquility of Saint Leo year-round.

Saint Leo College, the activity hub of the property, is a residential, four-year, Catholic, co-educational, liberal arts institution, founded in 1889 by the Order of Saint Benedict, and located about 65 miles west of Orlando. It has a fulltime student population of slightly more than 1,000—20 per cent of it made up of students from foreign countries, with a high concentration from the Caribbean.

A mile-wide, spring-fed lake abuts the north end of the campus. Orange groves border on the east and west; and the land to the south, once a cattle pasture, is now a golf course, leased from the abbey by an independent manager and open to the public seven days a week.

Over the years the role of the Benedictine monks here has changed. The cattle are gone. The groves are tended by hired help, and the fruit is harvested by buyers. As a consequence, the monks come into closer contact with the outside world, although they still adhere to vows of chastity, poverty and obedience. A number of the monks are priests and help out in nearby parishes. Some members of the order maintain a Pilgrim Center, which provides living quarters, meals and religious retreats for people of varied denominations. And for the monks there are always enough chores around their home to fill a workday.

The abbey and convent, incidentally, are not affiliated with the college—except spiritually, of course. The college is now run by a board of trustees.

Wrapped in a warm blend of Spanish baroque and contemporary architecture, Saint Leo is a comforting, instant retreat off life's busy, noisy highways. Walk the campus; rest here; visit the abbey church and grotto. It's a fitting atmosphere for vows and resolutions.

During the school year masses in the abbey church are generally offered on Sundays at 7 a.m. and 10:30 a.m., and weekdays at 4:15 p.m., but the schedule changes in summer. You can confirm mass times by calling the friendly public information department of Saint Leo College: (904) 588-8252 (weekdays) or (904) 588-8200 (weekends). Mailing address: Saint Leo College, PO Box 2314, Saint Leo, FL 33574.

The people in this office are public relations specialists, willing to furnish you with any information you need, and point you in the right directions on campus. Their office is in St. Francis Hall. Check with security at the front gate for guidance.

The Way to Go: West on SR 50, turn south on Interstate 75, and get off on Route 52 exit. Drive six miles east to campus. About a 130-mile roundtrip.

The Abbey Church, with its mellowed Spanish baroque architecture, is part of the tranquil St. Leo College campus.

Sarasota

Take a quick look at this bright, clean, graceful city with its flowered and landscaped bayfront, and its welcome shortage of gaudy commercialism. It's about all you need to understand instantly why so many writers and artists have chosen to establish permanent residence in Sarasota.

It's unlikely your first impression will tarnish after a deeper inspection of the mainland and the other three distinctive living areas: Siesta Key, wrapped softly by beaches, bays and waterway; Lido Beach, the best known offshore island of Sarasota; and Longboat Key, beautiful and secluded.

There is boasting from some quarters that Sarasota is "the cultural center of the South." Believe it or not, the statement gives an idea of what to expect here. There are sufficient tourist attractions to interest most travelers, but even for those with only the smaller part of a day to spare, to simply cruise around and look and absorb the atmosphere, the drive of two and a half hours from the Orlando neighborhood is recommended. It's a different Florida over here.

The 35 miles of beaches, to cite one difference, are not like those to be found, say, at Daytona Beach or New Smyrna Beach on the east coast where the brown sands are hardpacked by vehicular traffic. The beaches of Sarasota are white and powdery, gently sloping into the water. Although the waves of the Atlantic admittedly make a better scene for the surfing crowd, conditions here for swimming and fishing are equally as good. Better, some say.

Sarasota is situated on the Gulf of Mexico, approximately halfway down the west coast of the peninsula, 54 miles south of Tampa, 71 miles north of Fort Myers. Population: closest round figure is 50,000. Although the name of John Ringling is most often mentioned in discussions of Sarasota pioneer days, it was Bertha Potter Palmer, the grand dame of Chicago society at the turn of the century, who put Sarasota on the international map. Seeking refuge from a wicked winter in Chicago, she "discovered" Sarasota Bay and proclaimed it more beautiful than the Bay of Naples (Italy, that is; not to be confused with Naples,

Florida, 100 miles farther down the coast). The press in this country and in Europe picked up on Mrs. Palmer's words, and when she backed up her flattering claim by purchasing 140,000 acres of land in 1910, the Sarasota tourist industry was born.

Today, though, Ringling is the catchword in Sarasota. The renowned circus boss did more than quarter his "greatest show on earth" here in the winter. He bought property, drew up the city's first zoning regulations, and made a fantastic cultural contribution that still dominates Sarasota 60 years later. If you see only one attraction in Sarasota, make it the Ringling Museum Complex on the right side of US 41 as you drive in from the north, just beyond the airport and two miles before reaching downtown. Actually, it's three attractions in one.

First, see the Ringling Residence, called Ca'D'Zan, built on the 68-acre estate in 1925 at a cost of $1.5 million and constructed along the lines of the Doge's Palace on the Grand Canal of Venice. All the grandeur, inside and out, has been preserved. Fixed in a garden of endless roses, exotic plants and trees, it's one of the great homes of America. Home? Call it a palace.

By this time, Ringling had acquired the country's biggest collection of Baroque paintings from the 16th, 17th and 18th centuries, works created by such masters as Rembrandt and Peter Paul Rubens, so naturally he had to build a fitting museum in which to hang his treasures. The Ringling Museum of Art, a pink Rennaissance structure with a sweeping, restful courtyard, is indeed fitting. Picture postcard stuff. Be sure your camera is loaded.

Completing the complex is the Ringling Museum of the Circus, built in the image of a 19th century Parisian circus amphitheater. There are all kinds of displays here, telling the delightfully graphic story of the circus from ancient times in Rome to winter quartering in Sarasota.

John Ringling died in 1936, and left both museums and his home to the state. Admissions to the grounds are $3.50 (children under 12 free). The one admission price covers it all: one of the best attraction bargains in Florida. The complex is open every day, Christmas included. Hours: 9 a.m. to 10 p.m., Monday through Friday; 9 a.m. to 5 p.m. on Saturday; and 11 a.m. to 6 p.m. on Sunday. Telephone: (813) 355-5101.

At the Sarasota County Chamber of Commerce, 1551 2nd Street, on the right side of US 41 as you approach downtown, you can get details and directions to beaches, pa ˙ s and any of the other attractions, such as Bellm's Cars & Music of Yesterday, Circus Hall of Fame, Sarasota Jungle Gardens, Lionel Train & Shell Museum, Marie Selby Botanical Gardens, and the Asolo State Theater on the Ringling grounds (Florida's official theater troupe, performing in a charming 18th-century Italian court playhouse; call for play dates: (813) 355-2771.) Sarasota is also the home of the Kansas City Minor League Complex, and the spring training site of the Chicago White Sox.

Write for any information to Sarasota County Chamber of Commerce, PO Box 306, Sarasota, FL 33578. Telephone: (813) 955-8187. If the chamber is closed when you're in town, drop in at almost any motel or hotel for a current copy of "See Sarasota." It's a monthly listing of attractions and events.

The Way to Go: West on Interstate 4, then south on US 41 outside Tampa. Orlando to Sarasota: about 135 miles.

Atlantic Center for the Arts

You can almost hear the flow of creative juices when turning into this silent, heavily wooded hideaway.

And despite the focus on artistic contemplation and productivity, the welcome mat is always out for visitors.

Chartered in 1979, established with a grant from the Rockefeller Foundation and opened in May 1982, Atlantic Center for the Arts is located on the northern tip of New Smyrna Beach on Central Florida's east coast.

Master-apprentice is the basic concept of the center. Four times each year, in February, May, August and November, three nationally and internationally renowned artists of various disciplines are nominated by the Advisory Council to become masters-in-residence for three weeks.

Each master—playwrights, sculptors, dancers, poets, photographers, musicians, potters, filmmakers, composers and novelists—lives in his or her own one-bedroom cottage on the property. They lecture, conduct workshops, critique works in progress, hold readings, give recitals, exhibit and develop interdisciplinary projects with fellows (students) chosen by the masters themselves from applications.

The masters, most of them working on projects of their own, devote about 50 percent of their three-week stay with the fellows in both group and one-with-one learning situations. Some of them visit, perform and lecture at neighboring cultural institutions and schools.

Although several masters have accepted as many as fifteen fellows, groups of eight are about average. Tuition fee is $200, and the center helps fellows find convenient, reasonable living quarters in New Smyrna. Masters are paid an honorarium, food allowances and have use of a car. Poet-novelist James Dickey of *Deliverance* fame, one of the first masters-in-residence, lived here with his wife and infant daughter.

One of the more innovative enterprises, under the lead of sculptor Beverly Pepper, was installation of a 100-foot earthwork sculpture, constructed of plywood and reflective mylar, on the New Smyrna Beach oceanfront at Ponce Inlet Park in February 1985.

Atlantic Center for the Arts is open to the public weekdays from 9 a.m. to 5 p.m., and Sundays 2 to 5 p.m. Closed Saturdays and major holidays. No admission charge.

On the property, within view of a portion of Turnbull Bay, are three cottages, two workshop buildings and an administration building with gallery space. There's a new exhibition in the gallery every month, primarily the work of Florida artists. The modern buildings with rustic flair, designed by New Smyrna Beach architect William J. Miller, are linked with about 500 feet of boardwalk through the trees and sandy soil.

The second phase of the center, a theater complex, was targeted for completion at the end of 1986.

Artist/sculptor Doris Leper, a member of the board of trust-

Workshop buildings are hidden in the woods at Atlantic Center for the Arts. Photo by Martha V. Carden.

ees, is founder of the non-profit educational institution, which is still supported by the Rockefeller Foundation, plus the State of Florida and corporate and individual donors. Mary Jane Urban is administrative coordinator, and Holly Bivins assistant director.

More than fifty volunteers, mostly women, support the center in numberless tasks, and there's always a friendly face or two in the administration building ready to answer all your questions. If you're lucky, you might bump into a famous artist.

Recent masters-in-residence were playwrights Edward Albee and Ted Tally, composers Samuel Adler and John Corigliano, painters Lowell Nesbitt and Richard Anuskiewicz, poet Andre Lord, sculptor Duane Hanson, and writers Charleen Swansea and Raynolds Price.

For information about any aspect of the center, write to Atlantic Center for the Arts, 1414 Art Center Ave., New Smyrna Beach, FL 32069. Or call (904) 427-6975.

Driving down the snug exit road on the way back to the everyday world, you'll probably feel somewhat stately—and a bit smug—about the state of arts in the United States. This place is like somebody's pipe dream come true.

The Way to Go: From downtown Orlando, travel east on Interstate 4 for 35 miles to Exit 56 (DeLand-New Smyrna Beach). Take State Road 44 east to New Smyrna Beach (about 18 miles) and turn left (north) on the US 1 business route. Drive about five more miles and watch for Atlantic Center marker on right. Now you're less than a mile from destination. Turn left on to Art Center Road. Just shy of the deadend is the entrance, on the right.

Tarpon Springs & The Weeping Icon

Forty years after a marine blight nearly annihilated the sponge beds at Tarpon Springs, sponges remain the headline act in this town. Put it another way: If you don't visit the sponge docks, you haven't seen Tarpon Springs.

Oh, the sponge industry is nothing like it was in the first half of the century, when a small task force of Greek immigrants developed a fleet of 200 boats and more than 500 workers and turned Tarpon Springs into one of the world's leading sponge ports. Today you can just about count those colorful boats on your fingers, and some of these are busier with the tourist trade than with sponge diving.

Yet, the docks are still charged with strong strains of the old world and the old industry, and have been designated a National Historical Landmark.

Spongeorama on the docks is an ideal attraction for families, offering packed exhibition pavilion, gift shops, coffee shop in an authentic Greek Spongers Village, walk-through sponge boats and such. There is no admission charge to Spongeorama, although a small fee is charged at the theater if you care to watch a short, educational and entertaining film about the sponge industry and history. Taking in all that Spongeorama has to offer, one is inclined to feel quite the expert on the subject before going on his or her way.

The introduction of synthetics had as much to do with the maiming of the sponge industry here as that underwater blight. Real sponge, however, serves a variety of industrial and domestic needs today, and makes a unique art form.

Sponges are found in every ocean and from coastal waters to deepest sea. They are primitive animals—with no brains, no nervous systems—that eventually attach to rock or shell on seabottoms. Sponge does not burn and is nearly indestructible.

Tarpon Springs, virtually surrounded by the Gulf of Mexico to the west, was incorporated in 1887, a decade after its founding. It was an ideal resort town before the sponge industry came into the picture, and still is. A third of the estimated 15,000 residents are Greek, and the Hellenic culture is a major asset. The many and graceful bayous curling through residential districts lift the city aesthetically above the typical Florida community. Spring Bayou, site of the first settlements here, has grand, winding streets and gorgeous homes.

Tarpon Springs is a quiet blend of those old mansions, new subdivisions, marinas, motels, downtown and dockside shopping areas, antique shops, modern schools; and has its quota of modern industry. Residents and visitors have access to numerous white sand beaches, all the space needed for swimming, boating and fishing. And the town's reputation for distinctive cuisine, with a Greek flavor, from little restaurants to Louis Pappas' famous restaurant overlooking the sponge docks, is legendary.

Detailed information is available at the Greater Tarpon Springs Chamber of Commerce, 112 S. Pinellas Avenue. The ZIP is 33589. Telephone: (813) 937-6109.

Perhaps the most vivid and inspirational event at Tarpon Springs is the Greek Orthodox observance of Epiphany on January 6 each year. After lengthy morning services in the cathedral on this feast day, a procession moves at noon to Spring Bayou where the bishop blesses the water with a cross. After the blessing the celebrant casts the cross into the water, and young men of the Orthodox faith dive in with the hopes of retrieving it. A special blessing is bestowed on the retriever, and, according to legend, good luck will follow him the remainder of the year.

A festival of Greek food, music and folk dancing is conducted afterward, and there's a formal Epiphany Ball that night.

By all means, whether or not you're in town on January 6, visit St. Nicholas Greek Orthodox Cathedral and witness the Weeping Icon of St. Nicholas in the vestibule. The cathedral stands as a soft fortress of Greek culture and spiritual life at 36 N. Pinellas Avenue, within strolling distance of the sponge docks. Marble for this magnificent edifice, quarried in Greece, was originally part of the Greek Pavilion at the 1939 World's Fair in New York.

The Byzantine-styled structure, the pride of Tarpon Springs, with rich iconography, centered dome, carvings and chandeliers, is a replica of St. Sophia Church in Constantinople, and was named in honor of St. Nicholas, patron saint and protector of mariners. Completed in 1943, the church was elevated to cathedral status in 1976.

On December 5, 1970, a woman cleaning the church detected something unusual about the glass-encased painting of St. Nicholas: drops of moisture had materialized around the saint's halo! During the next few days several more parishioners reported sightings of "crystal-like droplets" on the icon. The pastor viewed the phenomenon for the first time on December 14, and the next day summoned a carpenter, who examined the glass case and declared it air tight. The painting was then turned to face direct rays of sunlight; but the "tears," as they are now called, continued to form.

A decade has passed. There has been no solid explanation or official sanction of a "miracle" by the Greek Orthodox Church. "Only time will reveal the message," the pastor has stated formally. Parishioners seem undecided about what all this means. Many of them touch the icon as they enter the cathedral. Many kiss it.

Even though fame of the Weeping Icon of St. Nicholas has spread, and thousands rushed to have a look, one gets the impression that the novelty has worn off. While visitors to Tarpon Springs swarm the docks and curio shops, and come to gape at the sun-wrinkled Greek men, and at the black-garmented Greek women walking the hill leading to the cathedral on Sunday, and buy their sponges, and taste their pastries, St. Nicholas stands a lonely vigil.

Are the tears real?

The Way to Go: West on Interstate 4. This highway becomes Interstate 275 between Ybor City and Tampa. Continue south on 275 into Tampa, and turn off at the Route 60 Clearwater sign. Turn north on US 19 and go another dozen or so miles into Tarpon Springs. Turn left at Tarpon Avenue.

Webster
Flea Market

Six days of the week, Webster is a quiet geographical subdivision of mid-Florida. But on Monday, this Sumter County town, hidden from the highway and located 49 miles west of Orlando, quakes with people and commerce. That's the day—and the only day of the week—the Webster Flea Market is open.

From its start in the 1930s as a one-shed farmers' product auction, the Webster Flea Market mushroomed into one of the biggest and most popular marts of this type in the southeast. Incalculable thousands of shoppers and browsers are drawn to each opening. Its huge covered sheds and its stalls are sprawled across more than 15 acres. Between 1200 and 1500 vendors are on the premises each week, hawking the edible and the wearable and everything in between.

Some folks regard flea markets as junkyards. Some flea markets deserve the label. Well, maybe the open-air Webster Flea Market has its share of throw-aways and scrubby items you wouldn't even hide in your attic or cellar, but these represent only a fraction of the long lines of goods available—the nostalgic, the necessities, the luxuries, the antiques. Prices climb from cheap to very expensive. You might have to do some serious snooping for a couple of hours or so to find what you want (or don't want, for that matter), but whatever you have (or don't have) in mind, it's probably here.

A bounty of plants, fresh fruits and vegetables, cheese, white and brown eggs, homemade sausage and other food too alluring to give the go-by, can be purchased in one of the big sheds. There's also a scattering of eat-and-drink stands, and restrooms. Parking on the grounds is free, but space is limited. Owners of the surrounding properties charge as much as $1 for parking, but you can lick this—if you're not against a bit of walking—by leaving the care out on the main street. There are no parking meters. The market is normally ready for business by daybreak.

Webster Flea Market is run by Sumter County Farmers Market, Inc., PO Box 62, Webster, FL 33597. Telephone numbers in the 904 area code: 793-2021, and 793-3551. Each Tuesday, starting at noon, a cattle auction is staged here, but compared to the Monday action it's only a sideshow.

Flea marketing can be fun if you're not allergic to adventurous shopping. In any event, you're on your own. Have a profitable day.

The old iron gate entrance to the converted Ybor Factory complex stands ajar, welcoming visitors to shop, browse and dine at the bazaars and restaurants inside.

Around the turn of the century nearly one thousand workers made cigars at the Ybor Factory in Tampa, some of whom are shown in this contemporary photograph.

The Way to Go: West on SR 50 about 45 miles, turn right on Route 471, drive another four miles.

Ybor Square, Tampa

Cigars put Tampa on the map.

The manufacture of hand-rolled cigars was once the city's only major industry.

The cigars were produced by the Latin population of Ybor (EE-bore) City, cranking up almost a century ago at Ybor Square, and now this location, close to downtown Tampa, is listed in the National Register of Historic Places. People here like to say that Tampa's newest attraction—Ybor Square—is 90 years old. Well, it's so new, all the restoration plans are not yet off the drawing board.

Finished or not, Ybor Square is ready for visitors. Fundamentally, the landmark site is three huge brick buildings which served as a cigar factory and the seat of the Latin Quarter's political and social life, converted into a neat, nostalgic, quaint place to shop, browse and dine. If your sniffer is in working order, you can catch the lingering aroma of tobacco, those faint souvenirs of the thriving industry established by Vincent Martinez Ybor in 1886.

Historical sidelight: It was from the steps of the cigar factory in 1893 that Cuban patriot Jose Marti made an eloquent appeal to the transplanted cigar makers to band together in the fight against oppression by the Spanish government in Cuba.

An attempt has been made to preserve every inch of brick masonry, grill work and wooden interiors of the original buildings. There's an arcade lined with gift shops and bazaars; a Nostalgic Market where you can find heirlooms, imports, antiques and an array of collectibles; a tropical garden patio; places to eat both American and Spanish food; and, naturally, a shop where you can watch craftsmen roll cigars.

Ybor Square reeks with charming atmosphere.

It's open Monday through Saturday from 10 a.m. to 5 p.m., and from noon until 5 p.m. on Sunday. Admisison and parking are free. The restaurants don't open until 11:30 a.m., and close at midnight. Address inquiries to the Manager, Ybor Square, PO Box 384, Tampa, FL 33601. Telephone: (813) 247-4497.

Ybor Square is only a five-minute drive away from downtown Tampa, the gateway to Florida's Suncoast, where you can easily and profitably spend the rest of your one-day excursion—and still not see a fraction of what the Hillsborough County seat has to offer.

Tampa, with a population close to 300,000, is the home of Tampa University, University of South Forida, Tampa Museum, Curtis-Hixon Convention Center, the Dark Continent at Busch Gardens, professional football Buccaneers, professional soccer Rowdies, art galleries, shipping docks, and, in the spring, the Cincinnati Reds of the National Baseball League. Tampa offers three pari-mutuel wagering sports: thoroughbred racing (January to March); jai-alai (December–May), and dog racing (September–December). Tampa has beaches, year-round outdoor recreation, nearly 40 hostelries, countless fast food stores (17 McDonald's Hamburgers locations, for instance), and more than 50 recommended restaurants, including the Columbia Restaurant which is billed as the world's biggest and finest Spanish eatery.

If you don't have to backtrack right away after visiting Ybor Square, drive directly to the Greater Tampa Chamber of Commerce in downtown Tampa at 801 East Kennedy Boulevard, and obtain all the information you'll need for a quick or leisurely inspection of the city. The chamber's visitor information hotline for current events is (813) 223-111. Or call (813) 228-7777. Mailing address: PO Box 420, Tampa, FL 33601.

Don't miss the Old Tampa Bay Hotel—a distinctive Tampa skyline landmark—which houses the University of Tampa today. At one time it was the state's fanciest resort hotel. In 1898, Teddy Roosevelt's Rough Riders were billeted in the hotel as they prepared for the charge up San Juan Hill in Cuba. Tampa's Fort Brooke was also an historic debarkation point in the 1830s as the United States government attempted to clear all the Seminole Indians out of the Florida Territory and ship them to reservations west of the Mississippi River. The attempt, as it turned out, was not wholly successful.

The Way to Go: West on Interstate 4. Get off on the 23rd Street (Ybor City) exit. The next street, 22nd, is one way north. You'll want to turn left at 21st Street, one way south. Continue south on 21st and turn right at the first stoplight. This is 9th Avenue or East Palm Boulevard. Turn left on 13th Street. Ybor Square is on the left, but there's an ample parking lot to the right on 13th. If you're going on to the Tampa Chamber of Commerce a mile away, head west on Broadway (7th Avenue), turn left on Nebraska, then right on Kennedy Boulevard. The chamber is across the street from the courthouse at the Kennedy-Jefferson intersection. Orlando to Tampa: 85 miles.

Major League Spring Training Camps

Twelve major league baseball organizations—and one from Japan—take their spring training each year within an easy day's drive of Orlando. Spring camps generally open around the last week in February and wind up about the first week in April.

The Minnesota Twins use Tinker Field at Church Street and Tampa Avenue in Orlando as their pre-season headquarters. The city-owned facility, incidentally, is named in honor of the late Joe Tinker, once an Orlando resident and the leading man of the fabled doubleplay combination of Tinker-to-Evans-to-Chance.

Tinker Field is also used by the Orlando Twins throughout the summer for a full schedule of games in the Class AA Southern League.

Closest major league camp outside Orlando is 20 miles to the south in Kissimmee. This is where the Houston Astros put their pre-season act together.

The other teams, their locations, and approximate driving mileage from Orlando:

Boston Red Sox, Chain O' Lakes Park in Winter Haven, 47 miles.

Chicago White Sox, Payne Park in Sarasota, 135 miles.

Cincinnati Reds, Al Lopez Field in Tampa, 85 miles.

Detroit Tigers, Joker Marchant Field in Lakeland, 55 miles.

Los Angeles Dodgers, Dodgertown in Vero Beach, 100 miles. The Tokyo Giants also train at Dodgertown.

New York Mets, Al Lang Field in St. Petersburg, 105 miles.

Philadelphia Phillies, Jack Russell Field in Clearwater, 110 miles.

Pittsburgh Pirates, McKechnie Field in Bradenton, 120 miles.

St. Louis Cardinals, Al Lang Field, St. Petersburg, 105 miles.

Toronto Blue Jays, Grant Field in Dunedin, 120 miles.

Pro Football
&
Swimming

Orlando Renegades joined the United States Football League in 1985, and play their pre-season and regularly scheduled games in Orlando Stadium (formerly the Tangerine Bowl), next door to Tinker Field, the baseball park, at Church Street and Tampa Avenue. The Renegades conduct their pre-season camp on a field adjacent to the stadium.

The New Jersey Generals of the USFL take their pre-season training at University of Central Florida.

Tampa Bay Bandits of the USFL and Tampa Bay Buccaneers of the National Football League play their games in Tampa Stadium, 85 miles to the west.

Vero Beach, 100 miles to the south of Orlando on Florida's east coast, is the pre-season camp grounds for the New Orleans Saints of the NFL.

Orlando is also the home of the Justus Aquatic Center, one of the finest swimming and diving facilities in the world. It's located on the southwestern rim of the city just off Interstate 4. Many state, national and international meets are held there.

Topical Cross Reference

GARDENS

GENERAL INTEREST

HISTORICAL

MUSEUMS

PARKS

SCENIC

SCIENCE

WILDLIFE/ANIMALS

About the Author

Edward Hayes writes the popular "Hushpuppies" column three days a week for *The Orlando Sentinel*, and contributes to its Sunday *Books* section. Born July 9, 1924 in St. Louis, Missouri, he served as an Army private, corporal and sergeant in New Guinea and the Philippines during World War II. He worked as an actor and at a variety of jobs before beginning his newspaper career in 1955, signing on as sports editor of the Blytheville (Arkansas) *Courier News*. He came to the Orlando newspaper as sports editor in 1967, and has written more than 6,000 sports and news columns, and countless feature stories and book reviews. Among his other books are several ghost-written biographies and a novel, *The Day of the Game*.